AN INTRODUCTION

Hunting Arizona's Small Game

AN INTRODUCTION TO

Hunting Arizona's Small Game

By Randall D. Babb

Arizona Game and Fish Department

Phoenix, Arizona

Published by
Arizona Game and Fish Department
5000 W. Carefree Highway
Phoenix, AZ 85086
www.azgfd.gov

Text: Randall D. Babb
Book Editor: Julie Hammonds
Designer: Susan Geer, Spiral Creative Services

Library of Congress Control Number: 2012944137
ISBN 978-0-917563-57-7
Printed in Canada
FIRST EDITION — DECEMBER 2012
22 21 20 19 18 17 16 15 14 13 12   1 2 3 4 5 6 7 8 9 10

Photo credits: George Andrejko (16, 17), Julie Hammonds (115, 117), Gary Kramer (42, 44), Bob Miles (author photo, back cover), Richard Ockenfels (57, 58), Bruce Taubert (109, 125, 127, 129, 131). All other photos by Randall D. Babb.

To my father, Dalton C. Babb, who taught me to love the outdoors and the things that live there; to the many good friends, four-legged and otherwise, who have taught me so much and with whom I have walked many miles and shared the field; and to those who came before us, the naturalists and explorers who first looked into this marvelous land and introduced the world to her secrets.

Acknowledgments

In many ways, this book has been in development for my entire life. I am grateful to many people who generously gave their time, knowledge, and friendship along the way. Foremost among them when it comes to hunting birds and other small game is Ken Crawford, to whom I owe a debt of gratitude. He has been the kind of friend and hunting partner most people wish they had. Because we learned together how to pursue many of the species discussed in these pages, this book is as much his as mine. Others who selflessly shared their knowledge and companionship on hunts far and wide include my wife, Candy Holod, as well as Kevin Clark, Trip Lamb, Bob Miles, Kelly Neal, Web Parton, and Jim Stone. I am grateful to Johan Marais for his friendship and knowledge, and for introducing me to African game birds: We have shared too little time in the field here and abroad. I thank biologist David E. Brown for time spent together in the field and his insights into Arizona's wildlife and habitats. The other Dave Brown (a hunting guide), Jon Hanna, Jim Heffelfinger, Craig McMullen, Leonard Ordway, and Web Parton reviewed sections of this book and made helpful suggestions that greatly improved the manuscript. Julie Hammonds provided excellent edits and guidance throughout the book's review. Without the help of these people and many others, this book could never have come into being.

–Randall D. Babb

About the Author

Randall Babb grew up hunting and fishing in Arizona with his father, Dalton C. Babb, a dedicated sportsman. And though Randy enjoys big-game hunting, his heart has always been with the pursuit of small game, especially birds. He has hunted birds all across Arizona, in many western states, and in parts of Canada and southern Africa.

He has written and provided photographs or illustrations for many publications, including *Arizona Wildlife Views*, *Herpetological Review*, *Journal of the Arizona-Nevada Academy of Science*, and *Southwestern Naturalist*. His book credits include contributions to *Finding Birds in Southeast Arizona*, *Gila Monster: Facts and Folklore of America's Aztec Lizard*, *Lizards of the Southwest*, *Snakes of Southeastern Arizona*, *Vampiro: Vampire Bat in Fact and Fantasy*, and *Venomous Reptiles of Arizona*, among others.

Babb started his biological career with the US Forest Service in 1983 and moved to the Arizona Game and Fish Department in 1986. He currently manages the information and education program for the department's regional office in Mesa.

Contents

Small Game Mammals

From Field to Table

Hunting Arizona's Small Game

Introduction to Hunting Small Game in Arizona

Arizona is blessed with a marvelous diversity of habitats, and these diverse habitats are home to a staggering variety of plants and animals. Many particulars come together to give our state such a wondrous assemblage of flora and fauna. Key among these are latitude, topography, and tropical influence.

Doves are one of the more popular Arizona game birds.

The pursuit of small game has the potential to take the hunter to some of the most remote and beautiful places in Arizona. Yet the hunting of many species, such as doves or squirrels, will most likely require only a short drive from home. Regardless, the variety available to the Arizona sportsperson is rivaled in few other states.

Though Arizona is not located on a major flyway, we receive an impressive variety of waterfowl. Here, the hunter may encounter ducks from nearly anywhere in western North America. Many relocated hunters make the error of disposing of their decoys and waterfowl paraphernalia when they move to Arizona, unaware of the opportunities they will miss. Granted, Arizona may not compare favorably to Nantucket Bay or the flooded timber of Arkansas, but it does support plenty of wintering and migrating waterfowl. Numerous rivers and creeks of all sizes provide migration corridors and habitats for waterfowl, and stock ponds, lakes, and seasonally flooded lowlands support ducks and geese of all sorts. It seems as if nearly every species flies through Arizona at one time or another.

A variety of upland game also inhabit Arizona. Rabbits are a numerous and underutilized game animal. Four species of tree squirrel haunt our woodlands from north to south. Numerous species of upland birds—including mourning and white-winged doves, quails, snipe, and dusky grouse—are available for pursuit in habitats across the state. When proper conditions prevail, Arizona offers the best desert quail-hunting opportunities in the country.

This book is meant to provide the hunting public with useful information for pursuing small game. Within these pages, a modest amount of biological and other information is provided for those interested in knowing more about the small game animals that populate Arizona. But the bulk of this text is geared to providing information the hunter, beginning or otherwise, will find useful in hunting a particular species.

This book is organized to allow the reader to find information on a desired topic easily and quickly. This first section deals with basic information, ranging from choice of gear to ethical behavior. It provides tips and ideas anyone will find useful when pursuing small game. The next two sections deal with particular wildlife species. Information is arranged in a stair-step manner, with increasing levels of detail at each consecutive level. Wildlife is separated into two broad categories: birds and mammals. These accounts are further subdivided by family, organized loosely by type and relationship to one another. After the species accounts, readers will find helpful guidance on how to take game from the field to the table, including game care and preparation.

This is not meant to be a comprehensive compendium of information on each species addressed. For more in-depth information on hunting techniques or a particular species or group of animals, visit the bibliography, where a number of excellent and informative works are cited. It is by no means an exhaustive list of literature, but it should be a good start for anyone wanting to learn more.

A Few Notes on Gear

The best gear is the kind that works for you.

There is seemingly no end to the variety of "essential" items available to the hunter. Small-game hunting is no exception. However, despite advertisements to the contrary, much of gear selection is a matter of personal choice. Often, what works well for one person does not suit the needs or preferences of another. The pursuit of game need not require a budget-busting investment in clothes and gear. Many everyday items can be commissioned for field use. An old pair of jeans will work as well on a squirrel hunt as a $200 pair of pants from the most elite sporting catalog. Despite popular trends, camouflage clothing is not required for hunting every species. Mammals, for the most part, are colorblind, and all but the most brightly colored clothing can be employed in hunting most species.

However, there are a few items that are not only practical but, in a few cases, may be necessary. Use of these items will enhance your enjoyment of your hunting experience. The following paragraphs offer several suggestions for your consideration. They are only suggestions, and it is up to you to decide what best suits your needs. No doubt, after a little experience in the field, you will identify other items you find handy and want to purchase. If possible, carefully examine the items before purchasing them. Try on the boots and walk around in them for a while. Make sure the game vest does not restrict your movements and the hat does not obscure your vision. Many sporting-goods stores readily accept returns, and you should not be shy about exchanging one item for another that better suits your needs.

Boots and Footwear

Pursuit of small game may require a lot of walking, often over uneven or rough, inhospitable terrain. It is important to find footwear that is comfortable and appropriate to your activity. Often, sportspeople give too little thought to their feet and take to the field with inadequate footwear. Once feet become sore or blistered, which can happen very quickly, a hunt is over. Good footwear is one of the most important items in the hunter's arsenal of gear. Unfortunately, good boots are typically expensive, but they will also last more than one season. A $150 investment in boots that keep your feet comfortable and protected for five or more hunting seasons actually costs about $30 a year (a rationalization my wife has always failed to understand).

Taking care of your feet is essential for happiness afield.

The primary question to consider before selecting field footwear is, what kind of hunting will you be doing? A pair of light shoes or boots is typically more than adequate for a dove hunt, where the hunter is largely stationary and the terrain is not difficult. However, a good pair of leather boots is the best selection for

Camouflage comes in a variety of patterns and colors.

negotiating the cactus-strewn, rocky hillsides inhabited by Gambel's quail. Cactus is an unavoidable hazard. If you walk long enough in desert terrain, no matter how careful you are, you will step into it. Leather boots offer the best protection. If you plan to hunt many different species, think comfort, durability, and foot protection. You will be far more comfortable on a dove hunt in a pair of heavy-duty hunting boots than you would be on a chukar hunt in sneakers.

Boots come in a variety of styles and configurations. They can be nothing more than robust tennis shoes made of canvas, or they can be knee-high leather affairs suitable to fending off charging razorback hogs. A good pair of Vibram-soled or similarly outfitted leather boots offers the greatest utility. Boots with higher tops (above the ankle) not only provide additional protection from cacti and rocks, but also give much-needed ankle support. The soles are also important. Generally, boots with an aggressive cleat design provide the best traction in rough terrain. Most boots require breaking in. It is wise to wear them around town for a few days prior to taking to the field on a strenuous hunt.

Game Vests

Game vests verge on being essential. They come in a variety of designs, but most have large front pockets for carrying ammunition and a spacious game bag in the rear for carrying birds, squirrels, rabbits or whatever other game is bagged. Game vests can be inexpensive and simple. On the other hand, recent innovations have produced models that sport water bladders, load-adjusting straps, numerous gear pockets, and so on. These can be staggeringly pricey.

Find a game vest that does not restrict your movements.

When selecting a game vest, there are a few things to consider. Perhaps most important is finding a vest that will not restrict your movements, even after it is loaded. There is nothing more frustrating for a hunter than wearing a vest that prohibits the full range of motion. A flushing quail is hard enough to hit when you're not restrained by an ill-fitting vest that restricts your swing.

I have never found the "perfect" game vest, but there are many models available that I like quite well. Features I look for are lots of pockets, water-bottle holders or a built-in water-bladder pocket, straps for tying a coat or sweater to the back, a blood-proof game bag with easy access, and durable construction that will hold up to catclaw acacia and other inhospitable brush. Personally, I prefer strap-style vests for numerous reasons. More often than not, hunting conditions in Arizona trend to the warm side rather than the contrary. It is not unusual to start a hunt bundled up in a coat and finish the day in shirtsleeves. Strap vests easily fit over any clothing from coats to T-shirts. But most important, strap vests typically restrict movements less than other styles do.

Selecting a Firearm or Bow

Part of the enjoyment and excitement of hunting any species of wildlife is the multitude of firearms available to the hunter. There are state and federal regulations that dictate the methods for taking wildlife, and it is important to consult them prior to hunting any species. For instance, in Arizona most birds can be taken only with a shotgun shooting shot, while either rifles or shotguns may be used for small game mammals. Even pneumatic rifles such as pellet guns can be used to take many species. These can be very effective on cottontails or other game of that size.

I encourage you to experiment to see which firearms you find most practical and enjoyable. As you advance in the sport, your tastes are likely to change—this happens to nearly everyone. Many hunters trend toward smaller firearms over time, to increase the challenge of the hunt as they become more seasoned. However, the need to efficiently and humanely kill whatever species you are pursuing should guide your choice of firearm size. In the species accounts, I suggest appropriate loads and

Shotgun actions (left to right): break-open single-shot, over-and-under double-barreled, side-by-side double-barreled, automatic action, pump action.

firearms suitable for hunting each animal. These suggestions are based on personal observation and experience and are meant to help you be successful and efficient.

Shotguns

Firearm selection is largely a matter of the pocketbook and personal preference. The majority of people attempt a "one gun for everything" approach when it comes to small game. This can work, but it also has its drawbacks. Most hunters use shotgun gauges far larger than necessary for the bulk of Arizona's small game. The 12-gauge shotgun is by far the most popular size in America. It is a fine firearm, but it is more than you need for almost all of our small game. In reality, there is no single gun that is perfect for everything, but there are some nice compromises that will fit almost every hunter's needs.

Shotguns come in four general actions or configurations: Single-shot, auto-loading, pump-action, and double-barreled (over-and-under or side-by-side).

- Single-barreled single-shot shotguns can be inexpensive, and are easy to use. Most are either break-open or bolt-action. This type of gun is a good choice for a child or the beginner who is shy about investing a lot of money early on.

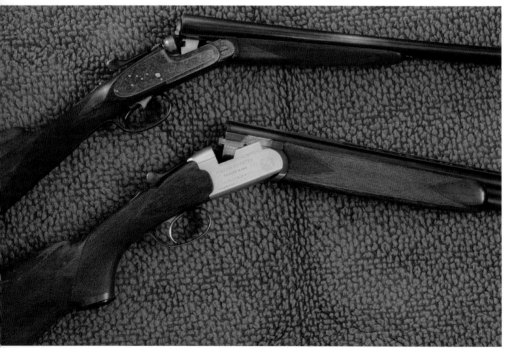

Double-barreled shotguns: side-by-side (top) and over-and-under (bottom).

- Auto-loading shotguns have actions that are run either by recoil or by gas captured from the expended shell. Most cycle ammunition very quickly with each pull of the trigger. As a general rule, auto-loading shotguns have less recoil than other shotgun actions. This makes them ideal for small-bodied shooters or for others who may be sensitive to recoil. Many of these auto-loading shotguns are light and easy to handle. Auto-loading shotguns can be finicky, though this is less a problem these days, due to the many improvements that have been made in recent years. Still, good maintenance is the key to keeping these guns functioning properly.

- Pump-action shotguns have a movable forearm that the shooter works to cycle shells through the firearm. These guns have the advantage of being very reliable, inexpensive, and easily serviceable in the field. They are one of the most popular shotgun designs in North America.

- Double-barreled shotguns typically have a break-open type of action and are usually pricier than their single-barreled brothers. These firearms, especially those with the barrels arranged on a horizontal plane (side-by-side), are more traditional in style. Side-by-side shotguns were some of the earliest types of shotguns manufactured. The more recently developed over-and-under barrel configurations (guns with the barrels stacked on top of one another) are more popular with American shotgunners than with European shooters. Traditionally, double-barreled guns are offered with double triggers. Each trigger operates a separate barrel, an advantage that leaves the shooter with at least one functioning trigger should there be a malfunction. However, most American shooters prefer single triggers on their firearms. Usually, each barrel of a double-barreled shotgun is choked differently (on models with fixed chokes). Combine this feature with a double trigger, and the appropriate choke can be easily and quickly selected with the pull of one trigger or the other.

A Few Words about Chokes: A choke is "an interior constriction at or near the muzzle end of a shotgun barrel for the purpose of controlling shot dispersion." The choke size is dictated by the amount of constriction. The greater the constriction, the tighter the choke. The choke is designed to concentrate the shot in the area of the target. The choke sizes most commonly encountered (from most open to tightest) are cylinder, improved cylinder, modified, and full. There are several sizes between these, ranging from skeet 1 all the way to extra full and beyond.

Much fuss has been and continues to be made regarding shotgun choke sizes. Most new guns have screw-in-style chokes that can easily be changed from one size to another. This innovation was revolutionary when it was introduced years ago, but is likely of little consequence today. There are still situations where shotgun chokes are truly important, but these are few in small-game hunting. I address them in the species accounts in following sections.

Chokes were first introduced as a means of compensating for inferior shotshell components, before the invention of cushioned shot-cup wads, high-performance powders, and buffered and plated shot. In those early days, shotshells had disk-like paper or fiber wads separating the powder from the shot. This unyielding wad configuration provided little cushioning to the shot as it accelerated from stationary to around 1,200 feet per second in less than the blink of an eye. This lack of cushioning led to pellet deformation: Lead pellets next to the wadding became flattened or otherwise disfigured, which caused them to not fly true. They would stray, sometimes wildly, missing the target by feet. This problem was further aggravated by those pellets on the edges of the shot charge, which became deformed when they rubbed against the barrel as they sped toward the muzzle. These problems were largely mitigated by several innovations, not the least of which was the integration of a cushioned wad with a shot cup. This minimized shot deformation.

With this and a surfeit of other advances, today's shotshells themselves do much of what chokes used to do. In fact, tests have shown that tighter chokes can be a detriment when shooting with today's shotshells, resulting in holes in the pattern or stray off-target pellets. In a nutshell, for most small-game shooting, a modified choke is as tight as you are likely to need. As a general rule, when considering today's modern shotshell loads, less choke is most likely better.

Choosing a Shotgun: A plethora of considerations should be given to any shotgun purchase. Probably the most important is how the gun fits YOU. Shotguns are pointed, not aimed. This makes the fit of a shotgun far more important than that of a rifle. When the shotgun is brought to the shoulder, the shooter should be looking directly down the barrel, and the gun should be pointing exactly where the shooter is looking. Your eye is acting as the rear sight, and it must comfortably and naturally align to the barrel when the firearm is quickly shouldered. Most shooters attempt to fit themselves to the gun rather than the gun to themselves. If a shotgun does not fit well, a shooter will never reach full potential as a wing shot. Shotgun manufacturers produce firearms in standard configurations that supposedly fit the mythical "average shooter." These standard-dimension shotguns seldom fit perfectly. Many production shotguns come with the stock slightly bent to favor right-handed shooters, which can be a big problem for left-handed shooters. This bending of the stock is referred to as "cast," and the cast is different for people who shoot right-handed than it is for those who shoot left-handed. Shotguns can be altered to fit a shooter's personal dimensions. If you find or have a shotgun you really like, consider having it adjusted to fit you. It will be money well spent. If you are considering the purchase of a shotgun, visit some sporting-goods purveyors and handle as many models of shotgun as possible. Select the model that meets your needs and budget, and fits you best. Additionally, consider the weight of the gun and what species you plan to hunt. Heavier guns tend to swing better and absorb more recoil than do lighter models. This makes heavy guns well-suited for hunting doves or other pass-shooting situations. Light guns are easier to carry long distances in the field, making them ideal for pursuing game species that require lots of walking, such as quail and chukar.

Most one-gun shooters select a 12-gauge shotgun. Ammunition for this gun is readily available, comes in a standard load of 1¼ ounces, is comparatively inexpensive, and is available in a great variety of shot sizes and loads. The 12-gauge is best suited for large, tough birds such as cranes, geese, and ducks, but it works well on smaller game species, too. A variety of different models are made by many

Standard shotshell sizes (left to right): 410-bore, 28-gauge, 20-gauge, 16-gauge, 12-gauge.

manufacturers, and some are fairly inexpensive. The disadvantage of 12-gauge shotguns is that they tend to be heavy and on the bulky side, making them difficult for small-framed individuals to handle and unpleasant to carry for long distances in the field.

The 16-gauge is considered by many to be the perfect gun for pursuing upland game. Many configurations can be quite light, making them a joy to carry in the field. The standard load is one ounce of shot, ideal for most game species. However, these shotguns are not a popular gauge, can be difficult to find, and typically cost more than other firearms. Ammunition is expensive and often difficult to find as well.

A personal favorite of mine is the 20-gauge shotgun. This readily available gun is offered in a variety of configurations, many very lightweight. The standard load for a 20-gauge shotgun is a ⅞-ounce load of shot. This works well for most upland game species. The smaller size of the gun and widely available, inexpensive ammunition make it a good choice for smaller-framed and

22-caliber rifles (top to bottom): semi-automatic, bolt-action, pump- or slide-action.

beginning shooters. The light weight of many models makes them easy to handle and perfect for carrying long distances. The variety of shot sizes and loads available in this gauge makes it suitable for all of Arizona's small game species.

The 28-gauge shotgun tends to be the choice for those seeking something a little different. This is unfortunate, as these small firearms perform very much like the 20-gauge. Many consider the load of the 28-gauge to be near perfect in its dimensions (the diameter of the shot charge in relation to the depth of the shot charge). Such dimensions make it a hard-hitting and effective load. These shotguns are far less popular than the 12- or 20-gauge, and ammunition costs about twice as much. The standard 28-gauge load is a ⅝-ounce load of shot. Ammunition is available in a variety of loads and shot sizes, but becomes ever more expensive the further one strays from the standard load. Like the 16-gauge, the shotguns themselves tend to cost more than other gauges.

The smallest shotgun commonly seen is the .410-bore (the only popular shotgun in the United States that is measured in caliber and not gauge). Its half-ounce load is less than half of the standard shot charge issued by a 12-gauge shotgun. This small shotgun, like its bigger cousins, is available in nearly every configuration one can imagine. The small size and light loads, which offer minimal recoil, make it very pleasant to shoot. These attributes make it a popular choice for youngsters and beginning shooters. In skilled hands, the .410-bore is a surprisingly effective firearm at ranges out to 20 yards. However, because of the lighter load and substantially smaller-diameter shot pattern (as compared to the larger gauges), more skill and practice are needed to attain proficiency with the .410-bore. Additionally, the ammunition is more expensive than the ammunition for 12- or 20-gauge shotguns, and its light shot charge makes it unsuitable for many species of game.

Rifles

There are relatively few rifles that lend themselves to the taking of small game. Probably the best-known and most widely employed of these is the .22 caliber. This small rifle has great advantages when it comes to taking much of Arizona's small game. Many .22 models are inexpensive, accurate, and cheap to shoot. These are effective for small mammals and work particularly well for squirrels and rabbits, but no small game birds can be legally taken in Arizona with this firearm. When selecting a .22, pick a model that fits your budget and needs, one you like that fits well. Many .22 rifles are lightweight and built on small frames, making them ideal for use by small shooters. You may also wish to outfit your .22 rifle with a low-power scope; squirrels can be devilishly hard to hit at the top of a pine with open sights. A scope allows the shooter to take full advantage of these small rifles.

Modern archery equipment barely resembles ancient bows and arrows.

Archery Equipment

Archery equipment is undergoing a near-constant evolution. What is found in most stores today only vaguely resembles the ancient weapon used so many eons ago. Bows can be had in everything from traditional longbow styles to multi-cam high-tech compound affairs. They are available in a great variety of sizes and pull-weights, making them suitable for people of all sizes. If this is an avenue you wish to pursue, find someone knowledgeable and ask for guidance. Most archery shops will be glad to guide you through the maze of equipment and options to help you find a practical and efficient outfit you will enjoy hunting with.

The Ethical and Safe Hunter

Common sense is really what ethical and safe hunting is all about. Many decisions or actions involving hunter etiquette are no different than the courtesies we apply in our everyday lives, things most of us should have learned from our mothers (had we been paying attention).

Hunting is about having an experience and spending time in the field, not about filling the game bag. Those hunts where the birds are abundant and the shooting is great are always memorable, but they are so because they are the exception rather than the rule. Hunting is really about getting away and enjoying time with friends, dogs, and nature. Take time to have fun, learn about the wild, don't get discouraged, and if the hunt isn't perfect, take it in stride.

For beginning hunters, there are hunter safety classes offered statewide every year that teach the basics of safe gun handling and hunting. These classes not only educate and inform the beginning hunter, but provide insights into hunting in Arizona for the seasoned sportsperson new to the state. The Arizona Game and Fish

Hunting is really about getting away and spending time with friends and family.

Department recommends that all beginning hunters take these courses, which are offered online or in classroom settings. A complete list of current hunter education courses can be found on the Arizona Game and Fish website at www.azgfd.gov.

Following are a few less intuitive rules of the field and some old standards that new hunters will find useful and old hunters won't mind being reminded of.

- First and foremost: Be safe, and have fun by being so. Be aware of your surroundings and the positions of all your hunting partners and dogs. Carry your firearm in a safe manner, and don't take risky or otherwise unsafe shots. A bird or squirrel is not worth the life of a friend.

- Pick up spent shotshell hulls or other ammunition. Many sportspeople who would go to great lengths not to leave a candy wrapper or other litter in the field think nothing of leaving spent hulls ejected from a shotgun. Arizona regulations state that it is a crime to leave spent hulls in the field—it is considered littering.

- Make a genuine effort to retrieve all downed or wounded game. Finding dropped birds in heavy cover can be very difficult at times. Carefully mark downed birds and walk directly to them.

- Don't crowd other hunters. If you hear or see another hunter in the field or find hunters in a spot you intended to hunt, move to another area. There is a lot of public land in Arizona, and there are many good places to hunt.

- Ask for permission before entering private land and respect the landowner's property. Many private landowners have sign-in boxes that allow sportspeople access to their lands. Be sure to sign in and out and report unethical behavior.

- Keep control of your hunting dogs. Don't allow them to harass livestock or wildlife. Steer clear of cows with calves or livestock around water.

- Leave gates as you find them. After you pass through, always close gates that were closed and leave open gates that were open.

- Don't get lost. Make sure to carry a GPS and mark where you parked your vehicle. If you don't have a GPS, note landmarks before leaving your parking spot and while you are afield.

- Last: Be careful. Avoid strangers along the border with Mexico, and report any suspicious activities.

Small Game Birds

Introduction to Small Game Birds and Bird Hunting

Arizona is home to a wonderful variety of game-bird species. Each winter, the Grand Canyon State is a destination for upland bird hunters from all across the United States, and justifiably so. On those rare occasions when the elements conspire to produce ideal conditions, our wing-shooting opportunities are unparalleled. But even in poor or average years, a hunter can pursue several species of birds.

Though Arizona is not located on a major flyway, a good number and variety of waterfowl pass through or winter here each year. Arizona has five species of quail and is the only state where Montezuma quail can consistently be encountered, making it a mecca for quail-hunting enthusiasts. Add some of the most robust mourning-dove numbers in the nation, dusky grouse, chukars, pheasants, band-tailed pigeons, several thousand sandhill cranes each winter, and white-winged doves, and you have a wing-shooter's paradise.

Arizona game birds are primarily hunted by four methods: pass-shooting, walk-up shooting, jump-shooting, and decoying. All methods offer their own challenges, and can vex even the most seasoned hunter.

- Pass-shooting is done by selecting a location where birds fly by and taking them as they pass. Doves typically are hunted in this manner. Pass-shooting can be tremendously challenging, and weather conditions such as high winds, which allow the birds to fly and maneuver more quickly, can humble the most adept shotgunner.

- Walk-up shooting is most often employed for hunting quail, grouse, and other flushing birds. The hunter takes to the field, walking into areas where birds are likely to be found. Dogs are a popular addition to this style of hunting, and can assist greatly in locating some species. Once birds are located, they are flushed from cover and taken on the wing.

- Jump-shooting generally is used when taking waterfowl from smaller bodies of water. Birds are located from a distance with the use of binoculars. Once a pond is determined to be holding birds, a stalk is planned. The quarry generally is approached from behind cover such as brush or the dike of a stock tank. Once the hunters have moved well within range, they emerge, jumping the fowl from their location and shooting them on the wing.

- Decoying can be done with a surprising variety of birds. It works well with most species that fly to and from feeding, roosting, and watering sites. Ducks and geese are most commonly associated with this style of hunting, but many other birds can be taken with the use of decoys. Regardless of the bird species being pursued, using decoys to attract game birds is executed much the same way. First, decoys are deployed in a location being used or frequented by the species sought. Hunters then conceal themselves nearby, within shotgun range of the decoys, and take birds as they approach the decoy spread. Use of decoys often is coupled with calls or other means of attracting birds.

Quail, Grouse, Partridges, Pheasants: Galliform Game Birds, Family Galliformes

Dusky grouse.

Gallinaceous birds are those species that resemble chickens in general shape and form. Their legs are typically short or of modest length, and their toes are well-clawed. These birds possess broad, rounded, powerful wings that can quickly remove them from danger. The sexes of many species are strongly dimorphic.

Due to their terrestrial proclivities, these birds are usually encountered on the ground, either alone, in pairs, or in groups called "coveys" or "flocks." Many species perch or roost in trees, while others essentially never perch in vegetation, and roost on the ground. All these birds typically would rather walk or run than fly. Nests usually are constructed on the ground under the cover of shrubs, grass, or other shelters.

Arizona is home to nine species of gallinaceous game bird. The wild turkey, masked bobwhite, Gambel's quail, scaled quail, Montezuma quail, and dusky grouse are all native to Arizona. One of these, the turkey, is classified as a big-game species, so it is not covered in this book. The masked bobwhite, which is an endangered species, is not open to take by hunters. Three more species have been introduced to the state: ring-necked pheasant and chukar (a species of partridge), both from Asia; and the valley or California quail, from the western United States.

Quail

Quail reproduction is largely governed by habitat conditions preceding the breeding season. The most important factor is rainfall of sufficient amount to produce green feed and subsequent vitamins for maximum egg production. This green-up also allows insects to proliferate, which enhances the survival of quail chicks. Other important parts of the equation are the number of birds that survive the winter to breed the following season (carry-over birds) and, of course, the amount of cover for the birds to use for nesting and protection from predators.

Interestingly, all of our quail species, with the exception of the masked bobwhite (which pairs in June and breeds the following month), follow the same covey breakup and pairing pattern. In late winter and early spring, the covey breaks up and males begin advertisement calls to attract mates. Eggs are laid in a nest that may be simple or elaborate. One egg a day is laid until the full complement is attained. The pair and their young form the nucleus of a new covey. Family groups are joined later by individuals or pairs of birds that did not breed successfully. Covey sizes vary considerably among species.

In all of our quail species, males are more abundant than females. This disparity between the number of males and females varies between species as the plumage differences between the sexes increase. In Montezuma quail, our most sexually dimorphic species, this male-to-female gap is highest. This sexual disparity allows female quail the latitude to select from among many males for those traits that best suit the needs of the species, thereby promoting survival of their offspring.

Three species of Arizona quail belong to the genus *Callipepla*. This genus's name was coined by German herpetologist Johann Georg Wagler in 1832 by combining the Greek word *kalos* (beautiful) and the Latin word *peplum* (robe or tunic). *Callipepla* means "beautiful coat."

Gambel's Quail *(Callipepla gambelii)*

Other Names: Arizona quail, desert quail, Gambel's

Name: The species *gambelii* was described in 1843 by naturalist William Gambel and named for him by Thomas Nuttall. The story is a bit complicated, but essentially, Gambel forwarded the observations from his western expedition to his mentor Nuttall, who encouraged the Academy of Natural Sciences to publish them. This quail was described in the report and was likely unnamed. Nuttall probably filled in the missing pieces and named this bird in honor of Gambel. The subspecies found in Arizona is the western Gambel's quail (*C. g. gambelii*).

Description: At about six ounces, the Gambel's is our smallest quail. Both sexes are gray, with red-brown patches streaked with white on the flanks, and gray legs. The belly is buff-colored. Both sexes sport a rusty cap with a black plume or topknot protruding from it. Females have a smaller topknot. Males have a black mask bordered by white and a black patch on the stomach just forward of the legs.

Habitat and Distribution in Arizona: Gambel's quail are birds of deserts, low-elevation grasslands, and scrublands, typically below 5,500 feet elevation. They are

found in the Sonoran, Chihuahuan, and Mojave Deserts,
in addition to many chaparral and pinyon-juniper habitats.
Common plants they may be associated with are saguaro,
mesquite, paloverde, creosote, bursage, grasses, hackberry,
juniper, manzanita, cholla, pricklypear, burroweed, scrub
oak, and wolfberry. Gambel's quail are found over much of
Arizona below the Colorado Plateau, sweeping northward
around the west edge of the plateau and following the Mojave Desert north of the
Colorado River.

Biology: Gambel's quail resemble and are closely related to California quail.
Gambel's quail first appeared as a distinct species around the beginning of the
Pleistocene, roughly 1 million years ago.

Gambel's quail reproduction is largely driven by the amount and timing of the
rainfall that occurs between October and March, our winter rainy season. These
rains, when sufficient, provide important green feed containing vitamin A and
phytoestrogens, which bring the birds into breeding condition. Understandably,
breeding periods following wet winters are the most productive. Despite popular
belief, there is no proof that Gambel's quail lay more than one clutch of eggs per year
when conditions are optimal.

Nesting typically occurs in the spring and is signaled by the mating call of unpaired
males. This single-note "caw" call is usually given from an elevated perch. In the
best years, calling may start as early as January, but it generally commences in late
February. Calling males run regular routes, visiting the same perches at roughly
the same time of day. They usually call for several minutes from each perch.
Peak calling activity occurs in the morning and again in the afternoon. A nest is
constructed beneath vegetation or other sources of shelter, and the eggs hatch
in just over 20 days. More than one female has been documented to lay eggs in a
single nest. Sometimes, "nest dumping" occurs. This is when only one hen rears
the young and the others go off and do who knows what, resulting in hens with
exceptionally large broods. But generally, both parents attend a nest, and the male
takes over incubation should something happen to the female. The peak hatching
period typically occurs in late April or early May. A hen may lay more than 20 eggs
in a good year, but less than half that number in a bad one. The average clutch size
for Gambel's quail is 12. In years with poor breeding conditions, Gambel's quail
may postpone nesting or prolong the nesting season, resulting in birds nesting

throughout the summer. Gambel's quail nesting late in the season, June through September, is a bad sign and bodes poorly for the number of birds the following winter. Young birds are nearly indistinguishable from adults by about 20 weeks of age. Banded wild birds have attained ages in excess of five years, but research indicates most birds live less than two.

The diet of the Gambel's quail varies throughout the year but includes succulent plants such as winter grasses and heron's bill (redstem stork's bill), seeds, pricklypear fruit (in the late summer and fall), mesquite leaves and flowers, and insects. These quail acquire most of their water from food. Though they do not need free water, they use it when it's available, especially when conditions are dry.

Habits: For quail, the well-being of the individual depends on group cooperation. When the covey is together, there are many eyes watching for potential danger. The covey flush is a confusing event that makes it difficult for predators, including the hunter, to select a single target. When a covey flushes, the birds make every effort to stay together. It is only when the covey is fragmented that the individuals stick tightly to cover until the group can reassemble. One theory about this behavior is that when a bird lands and can see other members of the covey, as happens when covey members land in a close group or an area with sparse cover, it has the confidence to keep fleeing, remaining in the safety of its peers. However, when a bird

The male Gambel's quail is more colorful than the female.

lands and does not see its covey mates, as often happens in dense cover, it becomes frightened and confused and instinctively hides until it can reunite with the others.

The Gambel's quail covey is fully formed by the early fall. Coveys are composed largely of family groups joined by adults who failed to successfully breed. These coveys may number from six to rarely more than 100 birds in exceptional years. Typical covey size, which depends on reproduction, ranges from 15 to 30 birds.

Large coveys are more commonly encountered late in the winter, when several groups of quail may converge on favorable feeding grounds and form "super coveys." Coveys are fairly sedentary, spending their lives in a relatively small area. Home ranges recorded for this species run from 19 to 95 acres. Gambel's quail roost in trees and large shrubs. The thorny branches and dense cover of mesquite, hackberry, and wolfberry are favored sites. Roosting often takes place along washes or ravines, where vegetation is heavier. Gambel's quail typically feed in the morning starting just after first light, and again in the mid- to late afternoon before roosting. Midday is generally spent loafing in sheltered areas such as beneath heavy vegetation, especially on hot days. These birds often can be found near stock ponds, rivers, creeks, and other water sources. However, it is not uncommon to find them far away from any water.

When feeding, birds spread out and forage by scratching and pecking at suitable items. Individuals usually remain close enough to maintain contact with their peers. A variety of soft chips, clucks, squeals, and purrs keep the covey in contact at these times. A sentinel bird may watch for danger from a suitable perch nearby. Birds typically scurry for cover at first alarm or may attempt to outrun danger. These birds usually take wing only when pressed.

Gambel's quail are capable of a variety of vocalizations. It is not unusual for the flush of a startled bird to be accompanied by a rapid cackle as it takes wing. One of the most commonly heard calls is the three-part assembly call, one that has graced the soundtrack of many a Western. Often given from a perch, it is a series of "ha" sounds with the emphasis on the middle note, which is the highest: "ha HA ha."

Hunting Tips: It behooves the Gambel's quail hunter to learn to recognize the various calls they make. These birds can often be located by listening for their calls. Start hunting early in the morning, when quail are most active and vocal. While walking in the field, stop frequently to listen for birds. An often-employed trick for locating Gambel's quail is to imitate their calls to induce them to answer. Using a homemade or commercially available quail call and listening for coveys to answer can save lots of walking and time. Quail calls may be purchased at sporting-goods stores for a nominal cost.

Once quail are found, attempt to split up the covey and work cover for single birds. This is where you're likely to get most of your shooting. Estimate the number of birds seen on a covey rise, and keep a close count of the number of quail flushed while working the area for single birds. This way, you can make sure you've worked the covey thoroughly. In other words, if you have searched through the area where the scattered birds settled and have only gotten up half the number of birds counted on the covey rise, you know birds are still in the

area and can work the surrounding cover accordingly. In years of poor reproduction, you are faced with pursuing older, "educated" birds, which tend to run more, flush at greater distances, and generally be a pain in the neck.

Once flushed, Gambel's quail often fly uphill or downhill (usually opposite the direction you are heading). When flushing uphill, Gambel's quail generally land just over the top on the opposite side of the hill from the pursuer. They also may fly over a hill and land at the bottom or near the bottom on the other side of the drainage. Occasionally, they fly much farther, even out of sight. Gambel's quail have the frustrating and uncanny ability to at times "magically" disappear. This can be quite puzzling, and no amount of effort by either man or dog will find these birds. There is really no defense against this cruel trick, and it is best, after sufficient effort has been made to locate the vaporized covey, to push on in hope of finding a more cooperative group of birds.

A common problem Gambel's quail hunters encounter is when these birds choose to outrun danger rather than hide and fly away from it when closely approached. Though this problem can never be totally resolved, there are a few tricks that will increase your odds of success. First, avoid hunting areas where the ground cover is so open that birds find few places to hide. Such habitat encourages the birds to run and flush at excessive distances. Second, keep pressure on the birds in hopes of splitting up the covey. Do this by unloading your firearm and trotting after the covey until you have flushed the covey enough times for the birds to be sufficiently scattered to hold. Then work the area for singles.

Once the birds are scattered and holding, you will flush more birds if you walk in a zigzag pattern through the cover, occasionally pausing for a few seconds. Waiting can be as important as walking, in areas where there is good cover and where you know birds are hiding. It is not uncommon to walk into an area, stop for a few seconds, and have a bird flush right behind you after you resume walking. Be ready for this. Attempt to read the cover and terrain to predict where birds may be hiding. Groups of closely growing shrubs, shallow draws lined with dense vegetation, or low thickets should be investigated. If you have a partner, develop a game plan and move through an area about 20 to 30 yards apart, covering the area thoroughly. If birds are holding tightly, it is not unusual to cover the same ground many times and still flush birds. Quail also often hold closely in inclement weather. I especially look for snowfall in Gambel's country. Over much of their distribution, this is a rare event. On occasion, Gambel's quail hunting can be quite productive when these conditions prevail.

A hunter with a mixed bag of Gambel's quail and cottontail.

When a bird is knocked down, stay at the ready for a second or two to make sure the quail is not crippled and does not run off. Also, mark downed birds carefully, walk directly to the spot, and retrieve the bird. If the downed bird is not found immediately, take the time to carefully search the surrounding area within a radius of about 15 to 30 yards. Gambel's quail are remarkably tough. Crippled birds will run down mammal burrows or into packrat nests, or hide in almost any suitable cover. Resist the temptation to shoot at additional birds once a bird has been downed. This will translate to fewer lost birds and more game in the bag.

Gambel's quail can be hunted easily without dogs, but dogs can be very helpful. Dogs are particularly useful for locating downed birds, especially ones that have secreted themselves in packrat nests or rodent holes. Dogs also can smell birds at great distances and lead you to quail you had no idea were around.

Gear: Good boots and a light gun: That pretty much sums up the primary needs of the Gambel's quail hunter. Shotguns (with open chokes such as improved cylinder and modified) in 28- to 12-gauge sizes work well for hunting these birds. Most shots presented by Gambel's are within 30–40 yards, though uncooperative quail can flush far out of range of any shotgun. Shot size No. 7½ works well in 12-gauge, 16-gauge, and 20-gauge shotguns, but hunters who prefer smaller guns such as 28-gauge will have greater success if they step up to No. 6 shot. A one-ounce load is not needed with this larger shot size, but it is difficult to find lighter loads in No. 6 shot. A .410-bore shotgun is largely unsuitable for Gambel's quail due to the often long shots, tough nature of the birds, and light charges of the ammunition. However, if the birds are holding tightly, this small gun can be quite effective on this species. The ideal shotgun for quail hunting should be light, point quickly, and be easily carried for miles through rough terrain. A bird-hunting vest to carry bagged birds, shotshells, spent ammunition, water, and sundry gear is important, also. Good Vibram-soled leather boots will be appreciated, as much Gambel's-quail country is rough and cactus-strewn. A broad-brimmed hat wards off the intense desert sun.

Other Species: Hunts for Gambel's quail naturally lend themselves to multi-species bags. Doves can often be hunted while afield for quail. It is not uncommon to have mourning doves flush within gun range from brushy flats or trees where they are feeding or loafing. Desert cottontails and black-tailed jackrabbits are frequently encountered in Gambel's quail habitat and can be taken opportunistically by hunters. Gambel's quail hunters may also want to check stock ponds for resting and feeding ducks. This can be especially productive after winter storms that bring ducks down from the high country. Remember that nontoxic shot is required for waterfowl.

With a little planning, the Gambel's quail hunter can take other quail species on the same trip. Euphemistically known as the "quail slam," taking all three species of huntable Arizona quail is a challenging effort. Scaled quail overlap with Gambel's quail over much of their southeastern Arizona distribution, and mixed bags of these two species are not uncommon. However, bagging the third species, Montezuma quail, takes much more forethought, as this bird's habitat preferences have little in common with those of either Gambel's or scaled quail. Generally, the hunter will have to travel to oak woodlands to take Montezuma quail. That being said, tenacious hunters can bag all three species on a single outing.

Scaled Quail (*Callipepla squamata*)

Other Names: blue quail, blue scaled quail, scaly, cottontop

Name: This species was named by Irish zoologist Nicholas A. Vigors in 1830 from specimens collected on the central plateau of Mexico. The specific name (the part of the scientific name denoting the species) is derived from the Latin word *squama* (scale) and refers to this bird's scale-like feathers. Two subspecies are found in Arizona: *C. s. pallida* and *C. s. hardgravei*. The subspecies name *pallida* comes from the Latin word *pallidus* (ashen or pale). Archeologist and ornithologist Lyndon L. Hardgrave is presumably the honoree for which our other subspecies is named.

Description: The scaled quail is the second-largest species of quail in the state, weighing in at just over seven ounces for a large adult male. It is felt-gray to blue-gray, with buffy underparts and throat, and a white-tipped crest on the head. White teardrop-shaped feathers adorn the sides. Feathers on the nape of the neck, breast, sides, and belly are dark-edged, giving the bird a scaled pattern. The sexes are nearly identical, though the male's throat is unadorned, while the female's is subtly streaked with small brown tick marks.

Habitat and Distribution in Arizona: Scaled quail are primarily birds of southeastern Arizona's Chihuahuan desert grasslands (ca. 4,000 feet elevation). They also may be encountered in lesser numbers in the grasslands of east-central Arizona (between 5,000 and 7,000 feet elevation) and historically ranged into other grassland habitats. Scaled quail are often found in association with perennial grasses, soaptree yucca, creosote, mesquite, burroweed, and cane cholla (walkingstick cactus). They seem to prefer rolling or flat habitats, but will venture onto the lower slopes of mountains. Historically, these birds enjoyed a much greater distribution in the state, before the degradation and destruction of much of Arizona's grassland habitats.

Biology: Scaled quail rely on both summer and winter rains for reproduction and carry-over. Peak nesting typically takes place between April and May (but may extend into September when conditions are dry). Lone males give their mating advertisement calls from elevated perches. The nest is constructed of grass, often lined with feathers, and sometimes has a roof of grass, too. It is located in a sheltered site, such as in a clump of cacti. The number of eggs laid ranges from five to 22, with an average around 12. Tended by both parents, eggs hatch in just over 20 days. The young grow quickly and reach adult size by about 22 weeks. Scaled quail seem less subject than Gambel's quail to dramatic swings in egg productivity. Rather, carry-over of adult birds into the following breeding year appears to be one of the most important variables in maintaining high numbers for this species. Studies indicate that survivorship of birds into the following breeding season is tied to the amount of rainfall between October of the preceding year and August of the breeding year.

Scaled quail feed on green vegetation and seeds such as tumbleweed, snakeweed, mesquite, spurge, fairyduster, and pigweed, among others. Agricultural crops are also utilized when available. Invertebrates such as ants, beetles, and other insects of particular importance to the fast-growing chicks are also taken.

Habits: Scaled quail form coveys in the fall, comprising twelve to 25 or more birds. As with Gambel's quail, the coveys are made up of a family group joined by adults who did not breed successfully, and sometimes by other family groups.

Scaled quail prefer open grasslands with shrubs less than three feet tall. These birds take to cover, such as thickets along washes, when disturbed or to loaf or shelter from extreme weather. They typically roost on the ground on low ridges and become active at first light. At this time, they begin feeding in a loose group and may spread out over several dozen yards. Foraging birds often move in the direction of water, but neither the covey, nor all individuals in a covey, water every day. When they do water, they often show up at the pond in midmorning.

Scaled quail are quieter than Gambel's quail when moving or feeding, but it is not uncommon to hear birds give a "chuck-chuck" advertisement call from atop a low perch. Scaled quail have home ranges of up to a square mile in size, though daily movements are much smaller. Individuals of this species have been known to disperse more than 60 miles from their place of capture.

These quail, even more than Gambel's quail, love to run and when flushed may fly great distances. Birds tend to move uphill during the winter, but still inhabit the lower slopes and bajadas of mountains.

Hunting Tips: Because many of the same strategies employed when hunting Gambel's quail can be used for scaled quail, this discussion of hunting tactics will by necessity appear a bit repetitive. However, note the differences and see the Gambel's quail account for additional information.

As with Gambel's quail, start hunting early in the morning, when the birds are most active and vocal. Begin your hunt along low ridges above washes and drainages to locate these birds. If the weather is windy or inclement, concentrate your efforts where birds are likely to find shelter, such as the lee side of hills or thickets. As with hunting Gambel's quail, the object is to split up the covey and hunt for single birds. The initial covey rise is likely to occur out of shotgun range. Carefully mark where the flushed covey lands, and follow up as quickly as possible. The object is to press the birds into flushing again and break them up into singles. The covey may need to be followed up several times before this is accomplished, and it may be exceedingly difficult to split coveys up due to this quail's propensity for running. Once the covey has been split up, search for singles by slowly walking in a zigzag pattern, paying particular attention to any cover that may hold birds. Pause frequently to allow the birds to become nervous. Though scaled quail can and will hold very tightly, be prepared for birds to flush at long distances, especially if they have been bothered before. If birds are holding tightly, kick shrubs and toss rocks into potential hiding places to encourage concealed birds to flush.

Scaled quail can be quite vocal and often can be located by listening for their calls.

Commercially purchased or homemade quail calls also can be used to locate scaled quail by soliciting an answer from feeding or loafing birds. While walking in the field, stop frequently to listen for birds and visually scan far ahead for running birds. Look for good perennial grass cover with few shrubs or other vegetation. Open grasslands with mesquite-lined washes are ideal habitats. This vegetation provides hiding places for scattered birds. Attempt to read the cover and terrain to predict where birds may be hiding. Work cooperatively with your hunting partner, and move through an area

Male and female scaled quail are nearly identical.

about 20 to 30 yards apart, covering the area thoroughly. If birds are holding tightly, it is not unusual to cover the same ground many times and still flush birds.

Scaled quail are every bit as tough as Gambel's quail and will run if crippled. Be prepared to shoot crippled birds again as they run off. Great care needs to be taken in these situations to ensure the bird is clear of other hunters and dogs. Mark downed birds carefully, walk directly to the spot, and retrieve the bird: Dead birds can be notoriously difficult to spot when lying in heavy grass.

Gear: The essentials for all quail hunters are pretty much the same: good boots and a light gun. Open-choked shotguns (such as improved cylinder and modified) in 28- to 12-gauge sizes work well. Scaled quail can at times hold incredibly tight, and open chokes are appreciated in such situations. As with Gambel's quail, most shots presented by scaled quail are within 30–40 yards. A shot size of No. 7½ works particularly well in 12- and 16-gauge shotguns. Stepping up to No. 6 shot in the lighter loads of 28- to 20-gauge shotguns will increase your success and reduce the chance of crippling birds. The ideal shotgun for quail hunting should be light, point quickly, and be easily carried for miles through rough terrain. Due to the long shots often presented, the bird's tough nature, and the light charges of the ammunition, .410-bore shotguns are largely unsuitable. However, on days when birds are holding really tight, it could be just the ticket. A bird-hunting vest to carry bagged birds, shotshells, spent ammunition, water, and sundry gear is also important. Wear boots that are durable and have good soles. Scaled quail often inhabit rocky malapai slopes where terrain can be tough on your feet.

Other Species: In Arizona, desert and eastern cottontails inhabit much scaled quail habitat. Quail hunters are likely to encounter them along brushy draws and washes. Black-tailed jackrabbits are also a common species in our desert grasslands. Gambel's quail overlap in distribution with scaled quail across much of southeastern Arizona. Though scaled quail tend to prefer flatter, more open habitats than do Gambel's quail, it is not uncommon to find both species in close proximity or even in mixed coveys. While hiking in the grasslands, it is not unusual for a hunter to find mourning doves loafing or feeding near thickets or along drainages. Waterfowl of all sorts may be encountered on desert stock ponds throughout the winter. Though nontoxic shot is required for the taking of waterfowl, it is well worth the extra effort to keep an eye out for these birds.

Montezuma Quail *(Cyrtonyx montezumae)*

Other Names: Mearns' quail, fool quail, harlequin quail, Massena quail

Name: This quail was named by Irish zoologist Nicholas A. Vigors in 1830 from specimens collected in Mexico. The genus name is derived from the Greek words *kyrtos* or *cyrto* (curved or bent) and *onyx* (claw) and refers to the bird's long, curved claws. The species is named for Aztec emperor and warrior Montezuma II. The Montezuma quail subspecies found in the United States and northern Mexico, *C. m. mearnsi*, was named by naturalist E. W. Nelson in 1900 for army surgeon–naturalist Edgar A. Mearns. This subspecies is generally referred to as Mearns' quail.

Description: This largest of Arizona's quail species may attain weights over seven ounces. The Montezuma quail is plump in appearance, with a short tail, blue-gray legs with long claws, and a modest crest. The beak of both sexes is heavier than that of other Arizona quail, and is black with a robin's-egg-blue lower mandible. The hen Montezuma quail is clothed in a cryptic array of browns, tans, cinnamon, and mauve with dark barring, and light stripes on her back and flanks. This coloration makes her nearly invisible in the terrain she inhabits. The male Montezuma quail is a perplexing combination of perfect camouflage and startling, if not gaudy, pattern.

The cock is colored much like the hen dorsally, but has a striking black-and-white facial pattern bordered by a black collar at the base of the neck. Black bars adorn the wing coverts, and the flanks are black with white dots. The breast is chestnut, giving way to black thighs and rump.

Habitat and Distribution in Arizona: Montezuma quail are primarily birds of woodlands that have a perennial grass understory. They may be encountered in appropriate habitats in the southeastern quarter of the state, roughly from south of Flagstaff east to New Mexico, south to the international border, and west to the Baboquivari Mountains. Though present, they are decidedly uncommon across much of the  Colorado Plateau and White Mountains. Montezuma quail reach their greatest abundance in the oak and mesquite grassland-woodlands of the southeastern part of the state, south of Tucson. They often are found in association with perennial grasses, mesquites, live oaks, manzanita, Apache pine, Chihuahuan pine, madrone, and mimosas.

Biology: Montezuma quail do not tolerate overgrazing. Areas of little grass will harbor few, if any, of these birds. Studies show that the removal of 40%–50% of grass height does not allow these birds to survive. Montezuma quail rely on the concealment provided by tall perennial grasses to avoid predators and for nesting habitat. They avoid predation by sitting very tight and waiting for danger to pass. This habit is so ingrained in the species that at times a bird will sit in plain sight until the last moment before capture before taking flight. This habit led to the common name "fool quail," which is seldom employed these days.

Montezuma quail pair up in the late winter or early spring, regardless of rainfall. Breeding male birds call from the ground. They produce a quavering, descending whistle, sometimes referred to as the "buzz call." Paired birds select territories and nest when conditions become favorable with the summer rains, typically June through August. Montezuma quail nest on the ground and conceal the nest in clumps of grass or leaf litter. The nest is lined with leaves, feathers, and grass, and is well-hidden. The average clutch size produced by these birds is 11, with a recorded maximum of 16 eggs. In years of poor nesting conditions, clutch sizes may be six eggs or less. Eggs hatch after about 25 days of incubation. Peak hatching usually occurs sometime in August.

Male Montezuma quail are the showiest of Arizona's quail.

Montezuma quail covey size is generally small, with the average being somewhere around eight birds in a typical year. In exceptional years, a covey may range upward of 15 birds. It is composed of a family group joined by pairs or singles that were unsuccessful at nesting. Montezuma quail feed on a variety of items, including the tubers of wood sorrels and sedges, acorns, seeds, beetles, and other insects. They dig tubers from the ground with their long claws, leaving a characteristic conical cavity. In years of exceptionally high quail numbers, these diggings can cover large areas and look like tilled, unplanted gardens.

Habits: Montezuma quail have relatively small home ranges of about 15 acres. These birds roost on the ground, typically in perennial grass cover. Roosts often are located in the bottom of draws, but hillsides, small cuts, and saddles feeding into drainages also are used. Roosting birds form a huddle or ring with tails pointing in toward the center of the circle.

At daylight, these quail start feeding, moving slowly out from the roost, often going uphill. Montezuma quail are very quiet, and calls of undisturbed birds are seldom heard outside of the breeding season. These birds typically hold very tight, allowing for close approach before flushing with a startled whistle. The flush of a covey is explosive, with birds flying in almost any direction. Usually, they fly only a short distance, darting between and around obstacles, before settling to earth again. They typically run a few yards before holding up after a flush.

In cold weather, Montezuma quail may congregate on sunny slopes. They generally avoid snow, if possible. They do not need free water, but will drink if it's available.

Hunting Tips: A dog, preferably one with a good nose and that is staunch on point, is a necessity for hunting Montezuma quail. In those rare years of exceptional bird numbers, they can, with some effort, be walked up without the use of a dog. Rather than running as other Arizona quail do, Montezuma quail usually squat and sit tight when faced with potential danger. These birds hold so closely that a hunter can pass within a few feet without being aware of their presence. The odds of finding birds on an average year without the assistance of a dog are remote.

A dog that retrieves is a bonus when hunting steep terrain.

Most Montezuma quail hunters prefer to start hunting in mid- to late morning, after the birds have laid down scent, making it easier for the dog to find them. Unfortunately, the best scenting conditions often are in the early morning and late afternoon, especially in dry years. Look for good perennial grass cover with a 30% or more canopy of live oaks, pines, mesquites, or a mixture of these. If grass is not present, birds will be scarce or absent. In years of exceptional reproduction, Montezuma quail may be found in nontypical habitats, such as far out into valleys away from oaks or mesquites.

Montezuma quail are most often found in or near the bottoms of canyons and draws. A good hunting strategy is for two hunters to move along slowly, parallel to each other: Position one along or near the bottom of the draw or canyon, and the other about halfway up the slope. Let the dog work between and above you. Keep an eye out for small, conical diggings beneath trees, near rocks, or along the lower edges of slopes. These indicate a covey of Montezuma quail has been feeding in the

area, and birds are likely not far off. Once the dog goes on point, position shooters to cover openings in the vegetation through which shots at flushing birds may be taken.

With this species, most of the birds are bagged during the covey rise, and flushed birds can be very difficult to re-locate. Mark downed birds well, as they are nearly invisible when dropped in tall grass; hopefully, your hunting dog will come in handy here. A covey or more per hour may be encountered with a good dog in exceptional years, but expect three to five coveys for a day of hunting in most years.

Gear: Good boots are essential, as Montezuma quail habitat can be steep and, at times, rocky. Due to the close-holding nature of this quail, most shots at flushing birds will be within 20 yards. Additionally, these birds are not nearly as tough as other Arizona quail species. For these reasons, shotguns with open chokes and light loads perform particularly well for Montezuma quail. Shotguns in .410-bore to 12-gauge sizes with standard shot charges of No. 7½, 8, 8½, or even No. 9 are all effective at bringing these birds to hand. A game vest with lots of pockets to hold bagged birds, water, and the plethora of dog gear one often carries into the field on Montezuma quail hunts is very handy when pursuing these birds. Lastly, a reliable, well-behaved bird dog with a good nose and lots of stamina is needed to ensure success.

Other Species: The eastern cottontail is the rabbit species most commonly encountered in Montezuma quail habitat. In late winter, mourning doves can sometimes be encountered in large numbers loafing in oak trees. The lucky hunter can take a bag limit of these birds with no additional effort. On occasion, Montezuma quail hunters may be fortunate enough to happen upon an Arizona gray squirrel. The seasons for the two species overlap in the early part of the bird season. As when hunting other quail species, opportunistic hunters will want to check stock ponds for waterfowl. Follow all regulations when hunting these birds, as the requirements for taking them go beyond those for taking quail.

California Quail *(Callipepla californica)*

Other Names: valley quail, desert quail

Name: This species was named by English zoologist George Shaw in 1789. *Californica* means "from California," the area where the first specimens were collected.

Description: Similar to the Gambel's quail in appearance, both sexes of California quail have a black plume (topknot), with the male's being larger. Male California quail also sport a black face mask edged in white. Both sexes are gray, though California quail tend to be more blue-gray than are Gambel's quail. Both sexes have brown patches on the sides overlain with white darts. The California quail differs from the Gambel's quail in the following ways: The cap of the male is a dull brown and the forehead is typically white; the patch on the side is dull brown rather than rusty brown; the belly is covered with dark-edged feathers that form a scaled pattern; and a rusty patch is found on the male's belly. California quail weigh about six ounces.

Habitat and Distribution in Arizona: Introduced along the
Little Colorado River in the 1960s, California quail remain in
this general area today, where surrounding unsuitable habitat
limits their distribution. They have since spread to many of
the Little Colorado River's tributaries near Springerville in the
White Mountains of eastern Arizona, between the elevations
of 5,900 and 6,200 feet. They often shelter in the dense
vegetation that chokes draws and drainages at these elevations: willows, wild rose,
Rhus species, saltbush, raspberry, and junipers.

Biology: Males begin breeding calls in March, and nesting likely begins in May and
June. The nest is a shallow scrape like those made by the closely related Gambel's
quail, and is constructed beneath shrubs or other cover. The average clutch size for
California quail is about 14 eggs. Incubation time is just over 20 days, and the clutch
is tended by both parents. As with our other quail, both parents rear the young.
Young birds mature quickly and are capable of modest flights at 10 days. By early
winter, young are the same size and plumage as adults. As with other quail, the
family group is the foundation for the covey, which is later joined by other birds.
The diet of California quail includes seeds, succulent annuals, berries, and insects.
California quail, similar to most other species of quail, have a 98% mortality rate in
the first three to four years of life. The maximum life span recorded for this species
is more than seven years.

Habits: Like other quail, California quail are most active and vocal in the early
morning and late afternoon. These quail usually stay close to cover, even when
feeding. During midday, California quail loaf in dense cover or beneath vegetation
that offers a canopy, which affords them protection from predators. California quail
prefer to roost in trees and large, dense shrubs, often near water. These quail would
rather run than fly, and take wing only when pressed. Then, most of the time, they
fly directly to heavier cover. Escape flights are often short, due to this quail's habit of
staying close to shelter. Once ensconced in a thicket, these quail can be very difficult
to dislodge.

Hunting Tips: Unfortunately, in Arizona, most of the area these birds inhabit is in
private ownership and unavailable for hunting.

In areas of thick vegetation, such as willow thickets along streams or creeks, the birds can be exceedingly difficult to flush. Walking through these areas can be nearly impossible. In instances such as this, flushing dogs such as Labrador retrievers work particularly well to encourage birds to leave cover and assist in finding downed birds. Position yourself at an appropriate vantage point and send the dog in to chase quail out. Carefully mark downed birds for collection once the action dies down.

California quail make a variety of sounds; many are very similar to those of the Gambel's quail and can be imitated easily with a commercially purchased quail call. Use these calls to locate birds in their brushy habitats. If you encounter birds away from dense vegetation, approach them from a direction that will flush them away from the heaviest cover. By pursuing birds in this manner, you increase the chance for the quail to take shelter in areas more accessible to you. The object is to split up the covey and hunt for singles, as you would when hunting Gambel's quail.

California quail look much like Gambel's quail.

Gear: A light, fast-handling shotgun is appreciated when hunting California quail. Shotguns with open chokes (such as improved cylinder and modified) in the 28- to 12-gauge sizes work well. Most shots presented by these birds are within 30–40 yards. Though a shot size of No. 7½ works well in 12-gauge, 16-gauge, and 20-gauge shotguns, hunters who prefer a 28-gauge will have greater success if they step up to No. 6 shot. A game vest that holds your quarry, extra ammunition, lunch, water, and other essentials comes in handy. Though the country California quail inhabit in Arizona is not especially rough, there are many rocky bluffs and outcrops along the Little Colorado River. Good, comfortable boots keep you in the field longer and make for a pleasant experience.

Other Species: There are few other small game species that occur in the same areas as California quail.

Masked Bobwhite *(Colinus virginianus ridgwayi)*

Other Names: bobwhite, gentleman Bob

Name: The northern bobwhite quail, *Colinus virginianus*, was described by Swedish systematist and zoologist Carl Linnaeus. The genus name was given by German zoologist Georg August Goldfuss in 1820. It is a Latinization of a Native American word, *colin* (partridge). The specific name *virginianus* means "from Virginia," where the original specimens apparently were secured. The subspecies found in Arizona, *C. v. ridgwayi,* the masked bobwhite, was named in 1885 by zoologist William Brewster of the National Museum in honor of his colleague R. R. Ridgway.

Description: The masked bobwhite is our smallest quail. An adult usually weighs less than six ounces. Arizona specimens of the female of this subspecies are virtually indistinguishable from those found in Texas. The female is brown and tan, with dark bars, buff dots, and an ill-defined, buff-colored face mask. The breast is mostly off-white, with dark streaks. The mature male is marked like the female on the back, but is rusty-red on the breast and sides. Though facial markings are highly variable, the male's face and throat are covered by a black mask, often with a white stripe above the eye and light flecks on the throat.

Habitat and Distribution in Arizona: The masked bobwhite inhabited subtropical grasslands punctuated with mesquite and cholla. These habitats have been greatly altered, if not destroyed, in most places where they once occurred. Historically documented in a very limited distribution in valleys and grassy mesas in the Santa Cruz and Altar Valleys south of Tucson, this bird is now extinct in the wild in Arizona and possibly Mexico. It presently is found only as a captive on the Buenos Aires National Wildlife Refuge at the southern end of the Altar Valley, where attempts to reintroduce the species to the wild have been unsuccessful.

Biology: Masked bobwhite coveys break up into pairs in late spring or early summer, and breeding begins in July. Nesting typically occurs in August. Success is closely tied to the quality of summer rains. Young appear in late August and early September. Observations noted clutch sizes of five to 15 young for this species. Food items include new shoots of annuals and forbs, seeds, leaves, flowers, and insects.

Herbert Brown collected these masked bobwhite specimens in 1896 and 1897 at Calabasas (south of Tucson).

Masked bobwhites were discovered in Arizona by pioneer ornithologist Herbert Brown in 1884. By 1900, less than two decades after their discovery, these birds were thought to have been extirpated from the state. Searches in Sonora, Mexico, in 1931 and 1937 found masked bobwhite to be fairly common. Subsequent efforts in 1950 found these quail to be scarce, and attempts to capture birds and establish a captive breeding population were largely unsuccessful. Only 25 specimens had been collected by that date.

Masked bobwhites were not seen again by scientists for 14 years, and were feared extinct. Biologists rediscovered the birds near Benjamin Hill, Sonora, Mexico, in 1964. This population was the source for later reintroduction projects, and all captive birds are descendants of these birds. Sadly, recent reports indicate this Mexican population has failed also, and the masked bobwhite may be extinct in the wild. Searches conducted in April 2012 in previously un-surveyed habitats north of Obregon, Sonora, Mexico did not locate any masked bobwhite. At the time of this writing, efforts to find this bird in Sonora continue. The masked bobwhite was a habitat specialist that favored dense subtropical grasslands, cultivated fields, and heavy escape cover bordered by shrubs and trees. These habitats are virtually nonexistent in today's Arizona.

Northern bobwhites in the eastern United States suffer an annual mortality rate of about 75%. This species probably has a maximum life expectancy in the range of five years.

Habits: Masked bobwhites, like other bobwhites, roost on the ground in a circle, tails pointed to the center. Roosts are in areas of dense vegetation, usually grass. Birds are up soon after sunrise and feed out from the roosting area. A seasonal movement by masked bobwhites from open, grassy areas to the savannah's interface with denser, woody vegetation takes place in the fall. Wintertime movements can be quite extensive, as these birds search out seasonal food sources. Masked bobwhite make the "bob white" whistle call for which this species was given its common name.

Hunting Tips: Masked bobwhites are a critically endangered species and are not open for hunting.

Grouse

Grouse are more-or-less chicken-sized birds found in North America, Europe, and parts of Asia. Some species can grow quite large, such as the sage grouse of the Great Basin of North America or the capercaillie of Europe. Only one of the nine species of grouse native to the United States is found in Arizona. Grouse are largely birds of northern boreal and prairie habitats, biomes that are extremely limited in the state's arid confines. The dusky grouse (recently separated as a distinct species from the blue grouse of the extreme western United States) reaches its southern distributional limits in the White Mountains of eastern Arizona.

Dusky Grouse (*Dendragapus obscurus*)

Other Names: blue grouse, fool hen, mountain grouse, gray grouse, hooter, pine grouse, pine hen

Name: The genus and species were named in 1823 by zoologist Daniel Giraud Elliot, a founder of the American Museum of Natural History. *Dendragapus* means "tree-loving" and is derived from the Greek words for tree (*dendron*) and love (*agape*). This bird was described by naturalist Thomas Say in 1823 from specimens procured while he participated in Major Stephen Harriman Long's 1819–20 expedition to the Rocky Mountains and headwaters of the Missouri River. The species name *obscurus* is Latin and means "dark or indistinct."

Description: A large bird, the dusky grouse has dark gray and brown (male) or brown (female) mottled plumage. Light-colored darts, spots, and streaks are present on the sides, wings, and back. The sexes are similar, and can be difficult to distinguish on the wing. The female is browner in overall color and has dark barring on the top of the head. The mature male is much larger than the female and may weigh more than three pounds. It has a broad, dark, un-mottled tail with light-gray tips. The male also has white-based feathers on the neck and a fleshy yellow comb over the eye.

Habitat and Distribution in Arizona: Dusky grouse are confined almost entirely to spruce-fir forest habitats above 8,500 feet in the White Mountains, Kaibab Plateau, and San Francisco Peaks. The San Francisco Peaks population is the result of birds transplanted from the White Mountains. Recent dusky grouse introductions with birds captured in Utah and on the Kaibab Plateau have been made near Chevelon Canyon on the Colorado Plateau. The success of these transplants is yet to be determined. Grouse are most often associated with spruce, fir, and aspen trees, and with gooseberry and raspberry bushes.

Biology: Dusky grouse occupy some of our state's highest elevations year-round. Birds spend the snowy winter months perched in spruce or fir trees, where their diet consists solely of the needles of these trees. In the spring, the birds descend and feed on the ground as the snow melts. In April, male birds begin to use long-established strutting grounds. Male dusky grouse do not establish a display area until the second year of life. Strutting sites are typically small, natural clearings in the forest, and often incorporate downed logs or other objects from which the bird displays. Strutting areas range in size from small, room-sized openings to up to two acres, and there may be several in a male grouse's home range.

The mating display of the male dusky grouse is nothing short of spectacular. This stout bird fans its broad tail as if it were a miniature turkey, inflates purple air sacs on the neck and a yellow, fleshy comb over the eyes, and displays to potential mates while giving a low hooting call. Strutting is punctuated by tumbling display flights. Intruding males are aggressively challenged by the resident bird and chased off. Cock grouse mate with several hens if given the opportunity. Late May and early June are peak periods of mating activity.

Female dusky grouse.

Hens generally start nesting in May and usually lay between five and 10 eggs. The nest typically is constructed in a sheltered situation, such as beneath shrubs or fallen debris. It is a simple affair, a shallow scrape lined with grass and conifer needles. Eggs hatch in about 26 days, and chicks immediately leave the nest under the hen's supervision. Male dusky grouse do not participate in rearing young. Chicks hatch in late June and early July and feed primarily on insects. Hens with young chicks select cover sites with vegetation heights greater than 12 inches. Family groups break up in late fall. Birds winter singly or in small, loose groups of up to several birds.

Dusky grouse in Arizona feed on a variety of greens, berries, seeds, and insects, including wild peas, raspberries, dandelions, aspen leaves, gooseberries, ants, and grasshoppers. Seeds make up a small portion of the diet. Insects are of particular importance to young birds and make up as much as 75% of their diet in the first few weeks of their life.

Dusky grouse can be very long-lived; in fact, they are one of the longest-lived of all North American gallinaceous game birds. Ages of up to 15 years have been documented.

Habits: In Arizona, adult male grouse spend most of their lives near their strutting grounds. Hens frequent mountain meadows and forest openings. Dusky grouse often congregate in areas where succulent forbs and berries are available, such as forest openings, old logging roads, and the edges of burns. When disturbed, dusky grouse frequently fly into the nearest tree, occasionally one devoid of any foliage. When perched in a large conifer, they are nearly impossible to spot amid the dense foliage and shadows. Once in a tree, they can sometimes be very difficult to induce to take wing, though this is not always the case. When they do flush, frightened grouse typically fly away from the opposite side of the tree from the encroacher. Once on the wing, grouse may fly and glide great distances, and typically are quickly lost to sight in the heavy woods. Grouse seem to prefer to fly downhill when escaping and often alight in another tree. Dusky grouse spend much of their time on the ground, foraging singly or sometimes in small groups, when conditions are warm. A flock of grouse usually comprises a female and her brood of young. Once snow arrives, grouse quickly take to the trees, where they spend the remainder of the winter.

Hunting Tips: Hunting dusky grouse can offer everything from taking incredibly difficult snap shots at birds flushing through dense forests to having a bird standing nearby acting more like a barnyard chicken than a wild bird.

In Arizona, grouse can be very difficult to find. Walking down abandoned logging roads lined by berry bushes, dandelions, and other forbs in spruce-fir woodlands in the early fall is a good strategy. Also investigate the edges of meadows, forest clearings, and the aspen-conifer interface. Grouse often frequent such places to feed. Grouse are most active in the morning and late afternoon, but spend most of the day on the ground if undisturbed. Loafing areas often are in the shade, beneath large spruce or fir trees. As autumn progresses, narrow your search to areas with dense spruce and fir stands, and hunt from one patch of trees to another. Move slowly, and take long pauses near dense stands of conifers where you think grouse may be sheltering. A dog is not necessary, as grouse typically flush when approached to within 30 yards or so. Watch for birds on the ground in the shadows. Their dark coloration makes them very difficult to see. If the grouse are in the trees, the shots can be very

Dusky grouse are nearly invisible on the forest floor.

challenging as they bail out of the top of a 60-foot fir and disappear. When flushing from the ground, they are noisy and quite exciting, and though their flight is not particularly rapid, the cover they inhabit quickly conceals them.

Gear: Brush pants may prove useful for pushing your way through berry thickets, but in reality, most dusky-grouse country is a joy to negotiate. The elevations will no doubt be high, and mountains don't have to be steep for thin air to take its toll. Being in shape makes the experience more enjoyable. Despite the dusky grouse's large size, it is not a tough bird and drops easily to a light shot charge. Any shotgun from a 28- to a 12-gauge shooting a standard charge of No. 8 shot will typically bring down any bird you encounter. Due to the dense cover of most grouse habitat, open chokes such as skeet or improved cylinder are most beneficial. A double-barreled gun with improved cylinder and modified chokes is a good choice for these birds. A game vest allows you to easily carry bagged birds and essentials while keeping hands free. Though the terrain is not particularly rugged, it can be steep, and there may be downed logs and other obstacles to negotiate. Good boots such as those you would use on a quail hunt are a smart choice for hunting these birds.

Other Species: Red squirrel and Nuttall's cottontail are the two additional small game species the grouse hunter is most likely to encounter in Arizona. Though band-tailed pigeons visit spruce-fir forests, they tend to leave them before the hunting seasons begin.

Partridges

Partridges are Old World gallinaceous birds that resemble quail in many ways. They are stout-bodied, have strong legs, and prefer to run rather than fly. Many species roost on the ground and rely on cryptic coloration and retiring habits for protection against predators. Only one species of partridge is found in Arizona: the chukar.

Chukar *(Alectoris chukar)*

Other Names: hill partridge, rock partridge

Name: British zoologist John Edward Gray named the chukar in 1830. The genus name *Alectoris* was coined by German zoologist Johann Jakob Kaup in 1829 and is Latin *(alector)* for "rooster or cock." The species name *chukar* is an onomatopoeia created from the sound they make.

Description: The chukar is a large bird when compared to a quail. Weighing up to 26 ounces, it is gray with cream-colored underparts and sides. Bold, brown-edged black bars cover the flanks. A distinct, black-bordered white mask extends through the eyes to below the throat. Beak and legs are dull red. The sexes are nearly identical and can be very difficult to tell apart. The male is slightly larger than the female and often has a blunt spur or tubercle on the legs. The spur is similar to, but less pointed than, that of a pheasant or wild turkey.

Habitat and Range in Arizona: Chukars are primarily found north of the Colorado River in the deep canyons on the eastern portion of the Arizona Strip, such as Kanab Creek and its tributaries. They generally are encountered in steep, rocky terrain at elevations between 4,500 and 6,500 feet. Plants with which they are typically associated include cheatgrass, sagebrush, and junipers.

Biology: Chukars are native to the Middle East, and birds used for introductions in the United States came from Turkey and other arid countries. Chukars form coveys in the early fall. Coveys are highly variable in size and can number from five to more than 30 birds. A covey is made of numerous adults and their young. Coveys break up in the early spring when birds pair up for breeding. Males court females with calls and by parading with one wing extended. Nesting success is thought to be determined by the quality of spring rains and the number of adults that survived the winter. The nest is a simple depression constructed in a sheltered location, such as beneath vegetation or boulders, and lined with leaves and twigs. Clutch sizes average around 12, with a recorded maximum clutch size of more than 22. Hatching typically occurs in May and June, after an incubation period of about 23 days. Peak hatching occurs in late May and early June. Though the male is in attendance during egg incubation, it is thought he does not assist in this task other than by defending the area. After broods hatch, adult males form bachelor groups, and do not assist in raising the young.

Insects are the main diet of the fast-growing young birds. Young reach adult size in 16 weeks. During warm months, water is very important to chukars, and they typically are never found far from it. In cooler months and wet periods, chukars are less reliant on permanent water and may range far from permanent sources. Cheatgrass is an important food, but tumbleweed, fiddleneck, heron's bill (redstem stork's bill), and insects also are taken, depending on the time of year and age of bird.

Habits: Speak to any chukar hunter, and he is likely to relate the old axiom: Chukars run uphill and fly downhill. Unfortunately, this is largely true. Chukars are wary, and often fly long distances when disturbed. It is not uncommon to see a flushed covey fly across a deep canyon or out of sight around the shoulder of a mountain slope.

Chukars mostly inhabit steep, often rocky, hostile country where terrestrial predators have little chance of catching alert birds. They run when alarmed, taking wing only when pressed. Watching chukars run uphill over boulders like rats from a sinking ship is a memorable and discouraging sight. These birds roost on the ground under shrubs or along rocky ledges and feed out from roost sites during the day.

Chukars are most active in the mornings and late afternoon. At these times, they often can be heard calling from bluffs along the upper edges of canyons. Chukars can be very vocal and emit a variety of calls, including the "chukar" call. Flushes usually are accompanied by a staccato cackle. Midday is spent loafing in lofty areas, from which they can easily spot the approach of potential predators.

Hunting Tips: A typical strategy employed by those who hunt chukars consists of walking mountain slopes and canyon sides about three-quarters of the way up from the bottom. Dogs are helpful if well-trained, and if they do not press the birds too closely. They are especially helpful if they retrieve. Wishing a retrieving dog were on hand is a common feeling after watching a dead bird plummet hundreds of yards down a steep slope.

Mark flushed birds carefully and follow up as quickly as the terrain permits. Individual birds separated from the covey often hold well and can provide exciting shooting. Often, a flushed covey will fly out of sight or across a deep canyon, making pursuit impossible. Commercial chukar calls may be helpful in locating coveys. Watch to ensure downed birds do not run off if they are crippled. Chukars are tough birds.

Gear: Strong legs, good boots, and a complete absence of common sense are the most important tools employed by the avid chukar hunter. Chukars are large, powerful birds and can be difficult to bring down. Many shots offered by these birds may be at 40 yards or better. For these reasons, shotguns shooting one-ounce loads of No. 6 shot work well. Though sometimes chukars hold very well, this is usually the exception. You will probably find a gun with a slightly tighter choke more useful. Firearms with modified chokes are a good compromise when hunting these birds. Double-barreled shotguns (choked improved cylinder and modified with a barrel-selection feature or double triggers) are perfect. You will appreciate a lightweight shotgun that is easy to handle: Good choices are 28- to 12-gauge shotguns with the proper loads. A game vest is a definite plus, to carry shotshells, gear, water, bagged birds, and splints for broken limbs. Good boots that offer lots of ankle support and have aggressive sole designs are essential.

Other Species: The slopes inhabited by chukars are in some places also home to Gambel's quail and desert cottontail.

Pheasants

Pheasants are gallinaceous birds from Asia. They come in a stunning array of varieties and colors. Even the more sedately colored varieties are nothing less than gaudy. The ring-necked pheasant was the earliest exotic game bird introduced into the United States, with releases taking place in the early 1800s. Today, the ring-necked pheasant is one of the most popular game birds in the United States, and hunters contribute millions of dollars to the local economies of the Midwest in pursuit of this sporty bird.

Ring-necked Pheasant *(Phasianus colchicus)*

Other Names: ringneck, Chinese pheasant, ditch parrot

Name: Swedish zoologist Carl Linnaeus coined the genus and species names for this bird in 1758. The common name is Old French (*faisant*) for "pheasant." But the scientific name is Greek, *phasianos* (pheasant), and hearkens back to the bird's Asian origins. The genus name comes from the ancient River Phasis (now renamed Rioni) in what is now the country of Georgia, though it is unclear if the bird was named for the river or vice versa (the former is most likely). The species name is derived from "Colchis," the area's original provincial name.

Description: Pheasants in Arizona weigh up to about three pounds. The hen is mottled brown and tan with dark bars and light streaks. It has a plain, buff-colored underside. Her tail, though long, is not nearly as long as the male's. Both sexes have barred primary feathers. The male is brilliantly colored in russet, gold, and dusty blue with a long, barred, golden tail. The head is green and has small tufts resembling ears. A red "cere" covers the face from above the eyes down to the cheeks. On some males in Arizona, a white ring encircles the base of the neck. The cock or rooster also has spurs, similar to those of a tom turkey. Many pheasants encountered around Arizona exhibit unusual coloration, different from the classic and consistent look seen in pheasants in Nebraska, the Dakotas, or other well-known pheasant-hunting areas. This aberrant appearance is likely derived from the captive origins of our birds.

Habitat and Range in Arizona: Pheasants were widely introduced into Arizona from 1913 to the early 1970s. Most of these introductions fared poorly. The only wild population of pheasants that is currently open to hunting with firearms is in the agricultural lands south of Yuma. Here, pheasants are agricultural pests, feeding on lettuce and other crops. This flat and otherwise arid and seemingly unsuitable place allows pheasants to thrive through the moist environments created by agriculture.

Biology: Male pheasants begin setting up breeding territories in the early spring, where they display to receptive hens. Courtship includes flutter displays and calling. The rooster accumulates as many hens as possible, usually around three, in a harem, then breeds with them. Nesting typically occurs in May. Pheasants select sites with higher humidity, such as agricultural fields or heavy vegetation. The nest is a simple, grass-lined structure and is well-concealed. The cock pheasant offers no assistance to the nesting hen or in rearing the chicks. Up to 17 eggs may be laid, but clutch sizes more typically number around 11. Eggs hatch in about 23 days. Most chicks hatch in late May through June. Chicks quickly mature, and by September are on their own. Most of the diet of pheasants consists of agricultural products, including lettuce, alfalfa, barley, corn, and other crops. Insects are an important food for young birds, but are taken less often by adult pheasants. Pheasants have been documented to live three to five years in the wild.

Habits: Pheasants are never far from cover and only reluctantly move about in the open. They frequent agricultural lands and adjacent heavily vegetated areas such as weedy canals and agricultural pump backs. Overgrown river-bottom lands adjacent to agricultural areas also are used. Pheasants roost on the ground in thick cover and feed out from roost sites during the day. They are exceedingly wary and quick to take cover at the slightest hint of danger. Pheasants are mostly solitary, but occasionally a small group of birds may be seen feeding in a loose group. Pheasants are strong fliers and may fly long distances when disturbed. Birds often run ahead of pursuers, taking flight only when the cover gives out or when pressed too closely. Birds are most active in the morning and late afternoon. They typically loaf in dense vegetation during midday.

Hunting Tips: Pheasants are hunted on a limited basis in Arizona. Hunters must apply to hunt through a lottery drawing and, if successful, receive two permits for one bird each. Hunters are given maps of areas open for hunting.

Pheasants can be difficult to find amid thousands of acres of agricultural lands. A good, close-working, flushing dog can be a tremendous help. If you don't have a dog to root through brush, find a partner who is willing to push through dense cover and flush birds for the shooter. If you have a few partners to hunt with, attempting "pushes" may be productive. Pushes are a common strategy employed by pheasant hunters in the Midwest. Station a couple of hunters at one end of a stand of cover and have them work toward hunters positioned at the other end of the cover who act as blockers, intercepting any bird flushed toward them.

Hunt places such as weedy canal banks, tumbleweed-choked fencerows, brushy fields adjacent to agriculture, and overgrown pump backs. Explore any place near agriculture that is overgrown and has sufficient cover to conceal birds. Cattails along ditch banks, pump backs, and ponds are favored haunts. Search for birds by glassing agricultural fields with binoculars from a distance to spot feeding birds. Be prepared for flushes at long distances while hunting. Crippled birds run great distances in a short time, and can be very difficult to retrieve.

Gear: Good pants with heavy facing (brush pants) are handy in negotiating dense, prickly brush. A shotgun with improved or modified chokes is preferable. Shoot a minimum of one-ounce loads of No. 6 or 5 shot for these tough birds. Pheasants are large and powerful fliers and can be difficult to bring to hand, especially when flushed at a distance. Shotguns of 20- to 12-gauge should be sufficient. Choose a firearm that points well and is easy to handle, as it does not take a startled pheasant long to get out of range. Good boots will be appreciated, as pheasant hunting often requires lots of footwork. Top off your hunting gear with a game vest with a spacious game pouch.

Other Species: The agricultural areas of southwestern Arizona are also frequented by mourning doves, black-tailed jackrabbits, and desert cottontails.

Snipe: Charadriiform Game Birds, Family Scolopacidae

The Scolopacidae family includes woodcocks, sandpipers, godwits, yellowlegs, curlews, and numerous other shorebirds. Members of this family, though diverse in size and appearance, characteristically have slender bills and forage along the edge of shorelines, probing the mud for invertebrates. The snipe is the only member of this family in Arizona that is open to hunting.

Wilson's Snipe *(Gallinago gallinago)*

Other Names: common snipe, jacksnipe, snipe

Name: French zoologist Mathurin Jacques Brisson coined the genus name in 1760.

Ornithologist George Ord, of the Academy of Natural Sciences, gave this species its specific name in 1825. The scientific name of this bird means "delicate hen." The genus and species names come from the Latin *gallino* (hen). The bird's common name was given in honor of Alexander Wilson, an illustrator and ornithologist of great renown who preceded Audubon. Wilson was a good friend of Ord.

Description: The Wilson's snipe is slightly smaller than a mourning dove, with an average weight of about 1½ ounces. It is mottled brown, tan, and golden above, with a short, ruddy tail. Light-colored feather-tips line up to form stripes on the bird's back. The underside is white, and the sides have dark bars. The face is buff-colored, with dark stripes extending through the eye and over the crown. Eyes are set far back on the head. The beak and legs are long. Sexes look alike, though the female tends to be slightly larger and have a longer bill.

Habitat and Range in Arizona: Snipe are found statewide in marshy habitats such as the edges of rivers, flooded fields, seeps, and occasionally around stock ponds. Plants often associated with snipe habitat are cattails, grasses, sedges, watercress, tamarisk, willows, cottonwoods, mesquites, and sycamores.

Biology: Male snipe arrive on their summering grounds in April and quickly establish breeding territories. Here they perform elaborate displays to potential mates. Courtship consists of a series of high, arching display flights that reach heights of 500 feet or more, followed by seemingly out-of-control, plummeting dives. The bird vocalizes during these flights, but the feathers produce additional sounds that enhance the display. About four dark-blotched eggs are laid in late April through May. Eggs hatch after 19 days of incubation. Both parents share in parental duties. Chicks grow quickly and reach adult size in about three weeks. They are capable of short flights within eight days of hatching. Migration to wintering grounds takes place in September and October and continues through November. Snipe show a high fidelity to wintering habitats. They use their long beak to probe the mud for invertebrates such as earthworms, snails, and insect larvae.

Habits: Snipe are inconspicuous and are seldom seen unless looked for. Their superb camouflage makes them nearly invisible in their wetland habitats. They feed along the shoreline and in shallow water, squatting and remaining motionless when danger approaches. They typically hold well, flushing when the intruder is within

A brace of snipe.

20 yards or less. They give a raspy "scipe" call when they rise, and though initially they fly in a straight line, they soon begin to zigzag, presenting a challenging target. They usually fly only a short distance and can be followed up without much trouble. Often, they travel in a wide arc, returning to the wetland not far from where they were flushed. They drop rapidly as they descend, making for a difficult shot. Often, snipe migrate on moonlit nights, appearing as if by magic in places they frequent.

Hunting Tips: Snipe are one of the most overlooked game birds in the state. Snipe are generally hunted by walking them up. Find suitable-looking habitat and walk just off the shore, searching for birds. You can often spot snipe before entering an area by searching the water's edge with binoculars. A flushed bird will often circle around, presenting you with a pass shot as it returns to the water. Check suitable areas often, as snipe are prone to appear and disappear suddenly in feeding areas. Snipe are classified as an upland game bird and steel shot is not required for taking them. But because these birds are typically associated with wetlands frequented by waterfowl, the use of nontoxic shot is recommended.

Wilson's or common snipe.

Gear: You will find a good pair of rubber boots make snipe hunting much more enjoyable, especially when faced with the icy, winter water of a flooded field or a river's edge. Hip boots are most practical in case deep water is encountered, but irrigation boots work well if some care is taken. Snipe are relatively small birds and are easy to bring down. Shooting light loads of No. 8½ or 9 shot through a .410-bore to 12-gauge shotgun (with open choke) works well for these challenging little birds. In the places snipe inhabit, there is a fair chance a hunter may get his gun wet, so leaving the pricey English side-by-side in the gun cabinet may be a good idea. A game vest makes carrying shells, other essentials, and downed birds easier.

Other Species: Snipe habitat is often good habitat for ducks and sometimes geese. Quail, cottontails, and doves are also attracted to the brushy areas that surround these wetlands and may be abundant at times. Snipe can offer a great plus for duck hunters. After a morning duck hunt, consider walking nearby marshy areas or other flooded, low vegetation in search of snipe. If you prefer to jump-shoot ducks, snipe are common visitors to stock tanks.

Cranes: Gruiform Game Birds, Family Gruidae

Cranes are found in both the Old World and New, and are among the oldest extant bird species, first appearing 2.5 million years ago. Many species are uncommon. Cranes are characterized by short tails and long, slender necks, beaks, and legs. The terciary feathers hide the tail when the wings are folded. In the United States, cranes often are confused with herons and egrets, with which they share a superficial resemblance. Cranes do not perch, roost, or nest in trees, all of which are common habits of both egrets and herons. Also, cranes are much larger than the other birds with which they may be confused, and typically fly with necks outstretched rather than folded back against the body. Only two species of crane are native to the United States: the whooping crane and the sandhill crane. The whooping crane is an endangered species, while the sandhill crane is an abundant game bird. In recent years, sandhill cranes have shown a significant increase in numbers in those populations that inhabit the interior of North America.

Sandhill cranes in flight.

Sandhill Crane *(Grus canadensis)*

Other Names: Canadian crane, little brown crane, crane, sandhill, grulla

Name: Swedish zoologist Carl Linnaeus described this species in 1758. The genus name *Grus* is Latin for "crane," and the species and subspecies name *canadensis* means "from Canada." There are five subspecies of sandhill crane currently recognized by biologists; three of these winter in Arizona. The greater sandhill crane (*G. c. tabida*), Canadian sandhill crane (*G. c. rowani*), and lesser sandhill crane (*G. c. canadensis*) all winter in the same habitats. The subspecies name *tabida* is from the Latin word *tabidus*, which means "wasting away, melting, or languishing." The subspecies name *rowani* is given in honor of Swiss ornithologist William Rowan.

Description: Like other cranes, the sandhill is a large, mostly uniformly gray bird with a long neck, beak, and legs. Occasionally, feathers on the wings, back, and sides are rusty-red. This is caused by staining from the iron-rich mud cranes sometimes use to preen. Legs and beak are dark. Sandhills range in weight from 5½ pounds to more than 14 pounds, depending on the subspecies. Wingspan can reach up to seven feet for the larger subspecies. The tail is short and not visible when the wings are folded. The adult has white cheeks and a red, fleshy patch on the crown of the head. A juvenile sandhill crane has a brown-feathered crown, nape, and back.

The three subspecies of sandhill crane that winter in Arizona look essentially identical, but differ in size and measurements and, to a lesser degree, in color. The greater sandhill crane (*G. c. tabida*) is the largest subspecies in the state, weighing roughly 11–14 pounds. It tends to be lighter in color and may stand nearly four feet tall with the neck outstretched. The Canadian sandhill crane (*G. c. rowani*) strongly resembles the greater in proportions. This subspecies generally weighs 7–11 pounds and is light gray. The lesser sandhill crane (*G. c. canadensis*) usually weighs from five and a half pounds to eight pounds and approaches three feet in height. It tends to be darker than the preceding subspecies and has a proportionally much shorter beak.

Habitat and Range in Arizona: Sandhill cranes primarily winter in three localities in Arizona: the Sulphur Springs Valley, along the Gila River near Arlington and in the Safford Valley, and the Colorado River from south of Bullhead City to the general vicinity of Cibola National Wildlife Refuge. Cranes prefer to roost while standing in open, shallow water such as that found in the Willcox Playa when it is flooded, but

they also roost on sandbars in rivers, in large shallow ponds, and on large, open, dry playas. They often feed in agricultural fields, but also use open grasslands and weed fields. Plants associated with sandhill cranes include tamarisk, mesquite, perennial grasses, tumbleweed, and agricultural crops, particularly corn.

Biology: Sandhill cranes are the only crane species that consistently frequents Arizona. As a general rule, the smaller the subspecies, the farther north it nests. Some lesser sandhill cranes banded on their wintering grounds in southeastern Arizona have been documented nesting in Siberia. In the western United States, greater sandhill cranes migrate the least distance between wintering and nesting grounds. These birds nest in Utah, Colorado, Idaho, Wyoming, and Montana.

Cranes form strong pair bonds and have elaborate courtship displays. Courtship consists of a series of elaborate leaps and struts by both sexes, complemented by calling in unison. The nest is constructed on the ground in a marshy area or shallow water and consists of a large mound of vegetation. Two eggs are laid in early spring

Sandhill cranes occasionally feed in desert grasslands near the roost.

and summer and hatch after 30 days of incubation. Both parents care for the young. The downy young cranes are referred to as "colts." Young grow fast and are essentially the same size as adults by the time of migration in September. Cranes are omnivorous, but feed primarily on plants as adults. Agricultural grain crops are of particular importance during migration. Insects such as grasshoppers also are taken and make up roughly 7% of the diet. Wild cranes have been documented living to ages of 15 years, though captive individuals have exceeded 24 years.

Habits: Cranes are often confused with other long-necked shorebirds, such as herons. Herons and similar birds tend to fly with the neck folded against the back, whereas cranes fly with neck outstretched. Cranes, egrets, and herons all fly with the legs extended behind. Cranes typically travel in flocks of two to more than 100 birds. Groups of three and four birds are likely family groups. Greater sandhill cranes tend to fly a little later in the morning and in smaller flocks than their smaller cousins.

Groups of sandhill cranes usually form long, undulating ribbons when they fly. These birds often are quite vocal. Cranes make a wide variety of calls, from croaks and creaks to trumpets and trills. These calls can travel long distances, and cranes are generally heard long before they are seen. It is not uncommon to hear cranes calling and after quite a bit of searching, to spot them wheeling as tiny specks, thousands of feet in the air.

Sandhills prefer to feed and stage in open areas where vegetation is low and predators can be seen easily. Cranes become increasingly vocal before leaving the roost in the morning. They take flight after daylight and head more or less directly to feeding areas. Sometimes, smaller groups stage in an area and then fly out in large flocks. After spending a few hours feeding, they typically head back to the roosting area. Occasionally, cranes fly out to feed in the afternoon, an hour or so before dark, but this is infrequent. They are exceedingly wary and do not allow close approach. It is common for cranes to circle, riding the thermal currents high into the air, before heading to their various destinations.

Hunting Tips: Currently, only one area is open to hunting for sandhill cranes: the southeastern corner of the state. The hunt is held in portions of Graham, Greenlee, and Cochise Counties. The Sulphur Springs Valley is the most popular of these hunting areas. Permits to take three birds can be had only through an application and lottery draw process. On all hunts, most of the land available to hunters is in private ownership. Respect private land ownership to protect your privilege to hunt there. It is important to ask permission before hunting. Disassemble blinds or any

Setting decoys is the best way to hunt sandhill cranes.

Lesser sandhill cranes settle into the decoys.

other hunt preparations you have made and pick up any trash or empty shotgun hulls. Leave the fields as you found them.

Sandhill cranes are challenging to hunt. The word "crane" could easily be substituted for "goose" in the old axiom, "It takes two days to kill a goose." Sandhill cranes are creatures of habit, and to successfully hunt them, you must know what they have been doing recently, which gives you a pretty good idea what they are going to do. Before hunting cranes, spend time scouting to determine their flight patterns and feeding areas. Pattern their movements at least one day before the day you plan to hunt.

Many people prefer to pass-shoot cranes, which can be done if adequate cover to conceal the hunter can be found in a place where birds are flying low into a field. Pass-shooting, however, often leads to high shots and crippled birds. The best and certainly most thrilling way to hunt sandhills is with decoys, in a manner similar to the one used for hunting geese. Commercially made sandhill crane decoys are sold at sporting-goods outlets, or you can make your own.

Cranes often feed in agricultural fields, and this is where most hunting takes place. Before the hunt, find a field cranes are using and mark their location in the field carefully. A good pair of binoculars is vital for this activity. Allow the cranes to leave the field of their own volition. Once the birds have left, construct a very discreet blind near the feeding site and place decoys in the exact spot where cranes were observed (or as close as possible). Place the decoys in a loose sickle formation with the farthest decoys within shotgun range, say about 30 yards distant. These decoys serve as markers to gauge the range of incoming birds. If they are over the decoys, they are in easy range. If they are well out past the decoys, say 20 yards or more, they are likely too far away to shoot at. It is easy to misjudge the range of these big birds. Do not place decoys close together in a clump, as this is the way nervous birds behave. Also, face the decoys into the wind, if there is any.

Ideally, the blind should be virtually invisible when observed from 30 or 40 yards. Old fencerows, irrigation ditches, and low, shrubby field edges are all ideal sites for a blind. The most common mistake crane hunters make is building conspicuous blinds. It is helpful to cut some vegetation or place a few tumbleweeds over the top of the blind so you are not visible to cranes looking down from high up or above. Layout blinds can also be employed with good success for this species, and have the added advantage of allowing the hunter to deploy decoys in the middle of the field where cranes feel most secure.

Be completely camouflaged and wear a face mask. Occupy the blind before daylight: Cranes typically show up not long after sunrise, depending on the distance between the hunting site and the roost. Some commercial crane calls sound good, but you can imitate the calls of sandhills with your mouth. Cranes have incredibly sharp eyesight and are much more wary than geese. Flagging with gray material or dried crane wings works well to attract the attention of birds when they are still far away. Call and flag to distant birds until it is obvious they have seen your spread, then hide the flags and conceal yourself in the blind. Flagging when the birds are close brings attention to you rather than to your decoy spread. They will not tolerate any

movement once they are close to the blind, and they shy away from suspicious-looking objects.

Sandhill cranes typically lock their wings at a long distance, sometimes more than a quarter-mile away, and glide toward a landing spot. Like geese and ducks, cranes approach a landing area by facing into the wind. They may approach a decoy spread, swing outward at its edge, and buttonhook back into the wind to land. Be patient and give the birds time to work. If there is no wind, cranes often approach the decoys in a direct manner, gliding in to them or parachuting in with cupped wings from higher up. If done correctly, most of the shots taken at sandhills will be within 30 yards. Cranes, even those coming into a field, are traveling much faster than they look. Be sure to lead them adequately. A good tip is to lead the head of the crane as you would a dove or a similar-sized target, and forget about the long neck and trailing body. The tendency of most hunters is to lead the body and not the head. Resist the temptation to shoot at high or distant birds. This will avoid crippling cranes that cannot later be retrieved.

Gear: Good camouflage with a face mask is important. You will find brown camo patterns particularly useful in the dry conditions of winter agricultural fields and borders. Reversible camo is ideal, if it can be had. For flagging, gray flags or dried crane wings placed on handles are handy tools. Decoys of some sort, whether homemade or purchased, prove very useful. Cranes are big and tough. Because they are considered upland game birds and not waterfowl, the use of nontoxic shot is not required. Unlike snipe, cranes are hunted in agricultural fields, where the use of lead shot presents no threat to waterfowl or other birds. A 16- or 12-gauge shotgun shooting 2¾ or 3-inch magnum loads of lead No. 2 shot is very effective at bringing down these big birds. If steel shot is used, BB-sized shot would be the best choice. Some hunters prefer to use a 10-gauge shotgun, and it does work well, but it is larger than needed when shooting at birds in reasonable range.

Other Species: The agricultural fields where sandhill cranes are typically hunted are also often visited by mourning doves, Eurasian collared-doves, and Gambel's and scaled quail. Eastern cottontails shelter in the weedy field edges. On occasion, ducks or geese feed in the same fields as cranes.

Doves and Pigeons: Columbiform Game Birds, Family Columbidae

Doves and pigeons are found worldwide. They are characterized by their strong, direct flight, with evenly spaced wingbeats. They typically have small legs and feet well-suited for perching. Some species are brilliantly colored and have elaborate feather crests or other adornments. Most, however, sport sedate plumage. Doves and pigeons often travel in flocks. These birds are notorious for their shoddily constructed nests. Both sexes typically look similar, often with only very subtle differences to betray their gender.

Arizona is home to five species of native columbiforms and two or more introduced species. The band-tailed pigeon, white-winged dove, mourning dove, ground dove, and Inca dove are all native species. The small Inca and ground doves are not open to take by hunters. The Eurasian collared-dove began showing up in Arizona around 2000 and is now well established. The similar-looking ring-necked dove is common in some urban areas. Feral pigeons are abundant in many situations

White-winged doves feed heavily on the nectar and fruit of columnar cactus.

and can be hunted year-round. There is no bag or possession limit on pigeons or Eurasian collared-doves.

Mourning and white-winged doves both belong to the genus *Zenaida*, a word coined by Carl Linnaeus as a tribute to Zénaïde Laetitia Julie Bonaparte, wife of French ornithologist Charles Lucien Bonaparte.

Doves

Mourning Dove (*Zenaida macroura*)

Other Names: turtledove, Carolina dove

Name: Swedish zoologist Carl Linnaeus named this species in 1758. The species name *macroura* refers to the bird's tail: *macro* means "large," and *oura* means "tail." The common name refers to the mournful sound of the bird's call. One subspecies of mourning dove is found in Arizona, *Z. m. marginella*. *Marginella* is derived from the Latin word, *margo*, meaning "border."

Description: A large adult mourning dove weighs just over four ounces. The bird is gray dorsally with a buff-colored belly. The long tail is pointed, as are wingtips. It has an inconspicuous blue cere around the eyes. An adult's feet are pink, and the beak is dark and rather small. Black spots adorn the upper surfaces of the wings and are conspicuous when the wings are folded over the back. A small black spot is located below and behind the eyes at the opening of the ears. Both sexes are similar. The female is only slightly smaller than the male. A mature male mourning dove has an inconspicuous dusty-blue crown and a purple cast to the feathers of the lower neck and breast.

Habitat and Range in Arizona: Mourning doves are found statewide. They reach their greatest abundance in desert lands and adjacent agricultural fields. Mourning doves favor thickets such as mesquite bosques or citrus orchards for nesting and roosting. Plants often associated with mourning doves are mesquite, paloverde, saguaro, tamarisk, creosote, bursage, tumbleweed, amaranth, and agricultural crops.

Biology: Mourning doves are one of the most common birds in Arizona. They may be encountered from conifer forests to our lowest elevations. Though doves have been known to nest every month of the year, this is not typical. They do, however, often begin nesting early, sometimes in January, and continue to do so throughout the summer. Conspicuous stiff-winged, gliding courtship flights precede nesting. Two eggs are laid in a flimsy twig nest, which is usually located in a large shrub, tree, cholla, or some similar situation. The nest is rarely constructed on the ground. Both parents care for eggs and young. The female incubates eggs during the night and early morning, relinquishing egg-tending duties to the male for the hottest part of the day. Eggs hatch in about 15 days. The chicks grow quickly and leave the nest in about 13 days. They stay on the ground, in the general area of the nest, where the parents continue to care for them for a short time. The adults then nest again and repeat the cycle. Up to seven nesting cycles in a single year have been recorded for mourning doves, but four are more typical for this species.

Arizona hosts both non-migrating and migrating dove populations. Non-migrating mourning doves are resident birds, more or less spending their entire lives within the state's borders. After nesting, migrating doves pass through or leave the state on their way to wintering grounds in Mexico. Migration typically occurs in the late summer and early fall. Migrating mourning doves winter in Jalisco, Michoacán, and Guanajuato, Mexico. Many of the birds that inhabit Arizona during the winter months come from the states to our north.

Mourning doves feed primarily on small seeds. The seeds of amaranth, portulaca, spurge, sunflowers, and other native weeds are utilized, as are commercial crops such as corn, millet, safflower, and sorghum.

Maximum life span for this species is somewhere around five years. However, the annual mortality rate for this species, due to a variety of factors including predation, is close to 50%.

Habits: Mourning doves roost in trees along rivers and in thickets, orchards, and similar situations. They fly out from these locations in the early morning to feed and water. Midday is spent loafing, often on the ground or in low bushes. Loafing sites may be near feeding or watering areas or, more often than not, some distance away. Doves feed again in the late afternoon. They typically return to the roost just before dark, after they have watered. Mourning doves feeding in desert areas often

water at stock ponds in the midmorning, and again in the evening just before roosting. Doves that feed in agricultural areas often water at irrigation ditches and similar sites. Doves tend to follow established flyways when entering and leaving feeding areas, roosts, and watering areas. Flyways often follow geographic features such as washes, field edges, roads, and canals. Changes in the weather often alter these flight patterns. During periods of unsettled weather, doves may fly later in the morning.

Hunting Tips: One of the most important aspects of dove hunting is doing your homework. The surest way to an unsuccessful hunt is to rely on what the doves were doing last year. Doves shift their habits and flight patterns in response to environmental conditions (food, water, roost sites, etc.). *Spend time scouting.* A few reconnaissance trips can pay off in great hunting.

Check agricultural areas for cut grain fields, or fields that may be cut in the near future. Feedlots may also hold numbers of doves. Mourning doves often utilize desert weed crops produced by summer rains. Abundant summer rains may have the effect of dispersing mourning doves, making them difficult to hunt. A good weed crop may also keep birds away from agricultural lands or other man-created food sources. Roosting and loafing sites can make for good shooting and should be watched for. Doves select densely vegetated areas for roosts. Mesquite bosques, tamarisk (saltcedar) thickets, and citrus groves are typical sites employed for loafing and roosting.

Doves establish flight patterns and follow them. For example, a grain field with lots of doves feeding in it will have a few spots that offer the best shooting. Watch tree lines, washes, canals, field corners, or other structural features birds may follow. Late-season doves frequently shift flight patterns and feeding areas, so the more spots you have lined up, the better your chances for consistently good hunting. Desert water holes can often offer spectacular late morning or evening shooting during the late season, a great way to combine dove and quail on a hunt.

Avoid shooting near thickly vegetated areas, such as alfalfa or cotton fields, to minimize lost birds. If you do hunt a place with thick vegetation, try to choose your shots so birds fall into open areas. Mark all downed birds and walk directly to them to minimize the chance of losing them. If you stand still, or sit or stand next to some sort of cover (a ditch, shrub, tree, telephone pole), birds will be less likely to shy away. Wearing drab clothing also makes you less conspicuous. *Ask landowners before hunting on private land.* Pick up all spent shells and shell boxes. Wait to clean your birds until you reach home. Don't leave unsightly messes and trash on a landowner's property. Help ensure the continued privilege of hunting on private lands.

Gear: The difficulty in hunting mourning doves is usually associated with hitting these sporty targets. They are not particularly tough birds and fall easily to the gun with a well-placed shot. This makes a wide selection of firearms suitable for taking mourning doves. Everything from a .410-bore, shooting standard half-ounce loads of No. 8 or 9 shot, up to a 12-gauge shotgun is suitable for these birds. Light loads work very well and are preferred for their minimal recoil as, often, many shots are required to bag a limit of doves. Open chokes provide shot patterns hunters find most effective for all but the highest-flying doves. Most shots presented by these birds are within 30 yards. A game bag to carry birds and ammunition and to store empty rounds is helpful.

Other Species: Many small game species may be encountered in the agricultural areas and desert lands that doves frequent. Desert cottontail, black-tailed jackrabbit, white-winged dove, and Gambel's quail are common in mourning dove habitat. If fields are flooded, waterfowl or snipe may be present. Near urban areas, Eurasian collared-doves may utilize the same food or water sources.

White-winged Dove *(Zenaida asiatica)*

Other Names: whitewing

Name: Zoologist Carl Linnaeus named this species in 1750. The species name *asiatica* is a reference to Asia, which is a misnomer, as this species is confined to the

Americas. One subspecies is typically encountered in Arizona, *Z. a. mearnsi*, named in honor of army surgeon–naturalist Edgar Mearns.

Description: Whitewings are a large dove, weighing more than eight ounces when grown. The wingspan can reach nearly 20 inches. Young-of-the-year birds at one month weigh between two and three ounces. Both sexes are similar, with gray-brown upper parts, buff belly, dark beak, and pink feet and legs. Whitewings differ from mourning doves not only by their larger size but also in having a longer beak and a more extensive blue cere around the eyes. When flying, white-winged doves can be identified not only by the distinctive white band on the wings, from which they derive their common name, but also by their slower wingbeat and squared-off tail tip. The male white-winged dove has a purple hue to the feathers of the neck and breast.

Range and Habitat in Arizona: Whitewings are primarily inhabitants of Arizona's desert upland and scrub communities. Usually, they are encountered within flying distance of saguaros, an important food resource. Whitewings often roost in citrus orchards or thickets along rivers and washes. Their distribution within the state ranges from the vicinity of Kingman and below the Mogollon Rim southward across the  state. Plants often associated with white-winged doves are organpipe cactus, saguaro, mesquite, paloverde, ironwood, smoketree, ocotillo, creosote, bursage, and agricultural crops.

Biology: White-winged doves are tropical migrants, generally making their first Arizona appearance in early to mid-April. Northern migration is timed to the flowering and leafing of desert plants such as saguaros and mesquites. Whitewings are powerful fliers. Some birds begin migrating south to more tropical climes in July, after nesting. The majority of adult birds have vacated northern and central Arizona by the time hunting season begins in September. Few whitewings winter in Arizona. Birds that nest in Arizona winter as far south as Oaxaca, Mexico.

Whitewings feed heavily on the nectar, pollen, fruit, and seeds of columnar cacti such as saguaros and organpipes. Seeds of many other desert plants also are taken, including those of ocotillo, jojoba, elephant tree, and various forbs. Agricultural grain and seed crops are often utilized by white-winged doves.

Male white-winged doves display to attract mates. This display consists of the perched bird leaning forward, cooing, and simultaneously fanning its tail and extending its wings vertically over its back in a rapid fashion. This display is performed in bouts, each lasting several minutes. Stiff-winged gliding displays are also performed. Nesting begins in late May. The haphazard nest is typically constructed at heights ranging from 6–40 feet in a tree such as mesquite or tamarisk. Thickets of tamarisk or mesquite are favored nesting locations. The average clutch size is two eggs. The parents share incubating responsibilities, with the male dove on the nest during the heat of the day. The eggs hatch after about 14 days of incubation. The young fledge at about 16 days. The pair may re-nest if the young fledge early enough and conditions are good (food is abundant).

Habits: The late summer whitewing's day begins early, when the bird leaves the roost in the day's growing light. It heads more or less directly to the feeding area, which may be agricultural crops or desert seed sources. After feeding, the bird heads to water, which is often a great distance away. It feeds in the morning and afternoon, and waters twice a day. It heads to the roost site at dusk, typically after watering. Birds may accumulate in large numbers at a roost.

Hunting Tips: White-winged doves can be problematic to hunt, not because they are so very different from mourning doves in habits, but rather because they usually have left much of the state by the time the September dove season opens. An area that held lots of whitewings a week or two earlier may be devoid of the birds on opening day. Birds that linger in the state longer are often the young of the year. Of 1,496 whitewings taken by hunters, which were examined over a six-year period at the Arizona Game and Fish Department's Robbins Butte Wildlife Area, 521 (34.8%) were adults. This is pretty typical for most of the southwestern portion of the state. Taking a large adult on an Arizona hunt is not an easy task. Southwestern Arizona offers the best opportunities for collecting a mature specimen.

As with mourning doves, *spend time scouting.* Know where birds are and have a good idea of where they will be in a few weeks. Check agricultural areas for cut grain fields, or fields that may be cut in the near future, and look for feedlots or dairy operations. Whitewings typically pick densely vegetated areas such as mesquite bosques, tamarisk (saltcedar) thickets, and citrus groves for roosts.

Like other doves, whitewings establish flight patterns and follow them. Look for topographic features such as washes that birds may follow. Desert water holes can often offer good shooting in the mid- to late morning, and again in the late afternoon. Avoid shooting where birds may fall in areas where they will be difficult

to retrieve. Mark downed birds and walk directly to them to minimize the chance of losing them. Stand still or next to some sort of cover, making birds less likely to shy away. Wear drab clothing to appear less conspicuous (camouflage is not necessary).

Ask landowners before hunting on private land and pick up all spent shells and shell boxes. Wait to clean your birds until you reach home. This avoids unsightly messes and trash that may be left on a landowner's property, helping ensure your privilege of continuing to hunt on private lands.

Gear: The primary difficulty in hunting doves is hitting birds as they streak by. Whitewings, like other doves, fall easily to the shotgun. A variety of firearms are suitable for taking doves. Everything from a .410-bore, shooting standard half-ounce loads of No. 8 or 9 shot, up to a 12-gauge shotgun are suitable for these birds. Light loads work very well and are preferred for their reduced recoil. Open chokes provide shot patterns hunters find most useful for doves. Most shots presented by these birds are within 30 yards. A game bag to carry birds and ammunition, and to store empty rounds, is helpful.

Other Species: White-winged doves share much of their habitat with mourning doves, Gambel's quail, desert cottontails, and black-tailed jackrabbits. Watch for these species, to enhance your bag. Adjacent to urban areas or stands of tall trees, Eurasian collared-doves may be found in the same areas as white-winged doves.

Eurasian Collared-dove *(Streptopelia decaocto)*

Introduction: As their name implies, Eurasian collared-doves are native to the Old World. There are many species of similar doves throughout Africa, Europe, and Asia. This is considered an invasive species, and it is feared that these doves, as their population grows, may compete with native species. Though not listed in the Arizona Game and Fish Department's regulations as a game species, the Eurasian collared-dove is a common bird and makes excellent table fare. There is a year-round season and no bag limit for collared-doves, which means that, with the purchase of a hunting license, a hunter can hunt these birds all year long. Couple the superb sporting qualities of these doves with a year-round season and good eating, and there is little reason why a hunter can't enjoy a day in the field any time of year.

Other Names: collared-dove, Eurasian dove

Name: Hungarian entomologist and botanist Doctor Emerich Frivaldszky von Frivald described this bird in 1838. The genus name *Streptopelia* means "dove with a necklace" and comes from Greek words for "necklace," *streptos*, and "dove or wood-pigeon," *peleia*. The specific name is a derivation of the Greek word for 18, *dekaokto*. This is a reference to a Greek legend about a sorely underpaid servant girl who implores the gods to let the world know she is being paid only 18 pieces (coins) annually. The gods answer her prayer by creating a dove whose call is *"dekaokto, dekaokto"* to let the world know of her plight.

Description: A large adult Eurasian collared-dove may weigh close to eight ounces, but the average weight of 73 birds taken in September near Phoenix was just over six ounces. This pale-colored dove may be gray, dusty brown, or even mauve above, with a lighter-colored breast and undersides. A black collar with narrow white borders adorns the nape of its neck. Its beak is black and feet are pink. A light-colored ring surrounds the red eyes. The moderately long tail is squared off at the tip. When the tail is folded and is viewed from above, it is colored like the rest of the bird. When the tail is spread, as when the bird is flying, or when the tail is viewed from below, the tail feathers are white with black bases. The covert feathers of the vent area are dusky gray. The primary flight feathers are nearly black. The flight of this bird is strong and steady. Its wingbeats are slower than those of the mourning dove. It resembles the white-winged dove and domestic pigeon when silhouetted in flight.

There are some indications that this species is hybridizing with the introduced African collared-dove (*Streptopelia roseogrisea*). The smaller African collared-dove is very similar in appearance to the Eurasian collared-dove but is typically paler in color and has white vent covert feathers and pale gray primary feathers. The African collared-dove is closely tied to urban areas and seldom strays into the field where it can be taken by hunters.

Habitat and Range in Arizona: Eurasian collared-doves are found statewide, usually associated with urban and urban fringe habitats. They seem to prefer large trees in open settings for nesting and roosting, a commodity in short supply over much of Arizona's wild lands. They frequent feedlots and agricultural fields adjacent to urban settings, where they feed on grain used or produced in these operations.

Biology: Eurasian collared-doves are an exotic species first documented in Arizona in the town of Eagar in 2000. By the time of the first observations, they were already nesting. They were soon discovered all across the eastern part of the state. This species was accidentally introduced to the Bahamas in the early 1970s, and had jumped to nearby Florida by the early 1980s. It spread quickly across continental North America and now can be found from Alaska to southern Mexico. Numbers in Arizona have risen dramatically, and Eurasian collared-doves now are one of the most commonly sighted doves in many urban areas. If the current rate of expansion continues, they will soon be found throughout the Americas.

This species has a long nesting season that begins as early as February and continues

into October in Arizona. There is some evidence these birds may breed year-round in warm climates if plenty of food is available. Courtship displays consist of raspy cooing, fanned tail displays, and locked-winged, arching flights. Two eggs are laid in a flimsy twig nest typical of those made by other species of dove. The male brings the female material, and she incorporates it into the nest, which is typically constructed well off the ground. A nest location 10–40 feet above the ground is preferred and is used for multiple clutches. Incubation lasts around 15 days, and both parents care for the hatchlings. The young fledge in 15–20 days and, as with mourning doves, are attended to outside the nest for another week or more. Eurasian collared-doves have been documented to lay a new pair of eggs while still attending chicks in the nest. A single pair may rear up to 12 young a season in six different broods. Breeding birds are resident to the area in which they nest. Young birds disperse outward from their birthplace and may travel great distances to colonize new areas.

Eurasian collared-doves feed on a variety of seed crops. They frequent agricultural areas adjacent to urban areas and feed on grains such as maize, safflower, sunflower, corn, and millet. Presumably, they feed on the seeds of weeds such as amaranth and spurge, as do other dove species, but this has yet to be documented in Arizona. These doves also are common visitors to urban bird feeders.

Initially, there was a great deal of concern about how these invaders would impact native dove populations. To date, they seem to be having little discernible impact on mourning or white-winged dove populations, but the author did observe a nesting-site dispute between a collared-dove and mourning dove. Presently, it appears as though Eurasian collared-doves may occupy a niche between feral pigeons and wild doves. However, as numbers of these birds continue to increase and populations reach saturation levels, this species may start to displace native doves, or compete for nesting, roosting, or food resources.

Habits: Eurasian collared-doves behave much like other doves. They tend to fly a little later in the morning than mourning doves. Eurasians leave the perch after sunup and fly to feeding and watering areas. These sites typically are close to, or in, urban areas or situations with large trees where birds can find nesting and roosting habitat. After feeding, they move to watering and loafing sites. These are often close to the feeding area. Loafing situations may consist of thickets; groups of large trees such as pecan groves; windbreaks; or barns, silos, or other manmade structures. Midday is spent loafing, punctuated by occasional short flights. The birds leave their loafing site and fly out to feed again in the mid- to late afternoon. They travel back to the roost well before sundown, much earlier than do mourning doves. Like other doves, they use flyways to travel to and from feeding, watering, loafing, and roosting sites. These flyways appear to be less well-delineated than those of mourning or white-winged doves.

Hunting Tips: Scout potential roost, loafing, feeding, and watering areas adjacent to urban settings for these birds. Also pay attention to other places the birds may be using, such as abandoned farms or locations where large trees are present. The best time to scout for Eurasian collared-doves is when they are most active. Confine your search time from about an hour after sunrise to midmorning, and again the last few hours of the day. Watch for birds moving in and out of potential hunting areas and determine a locality that would offer the best shooting by patterning their comings and goings. When hunting, station yourself near some object such as a tree or power pole to break up your outline. Remain motionless until the bird has approached well within gun range. Take to the field about sunrise or just prior to it, and again in the last few hours of the day. Be sure you have the bird properly identified before shooting, as they can easily be confused with other dove species.

Gear: Eurasian collared-doves can be taken with a variety of shotgun gauges. A 12- or 16-gauge shotgun is certainly larger than necessary, but performs admirably on this species. Shotguns of 20-gauge size down to .410-bore are more than adequate. Standard loads of No. 8 shot down to No. 9 shot in larger gauges perform well. Use No. 8 shot in smaller firearms. Shotguns choked from skeet to modified should work well in most situations. A game vest to hold ammunition and to carry bagged birds will be a welcome addition to the gear.

Other Species: The mourning dove is the game species most often associated with collared-doves. In urban-fringe areas, Gambel's quail, desert cottontail, and white-winged dove may also use many of the same habitats to loaf, roost, feed, or water.

Pigeons

Band-tailed Pigeon (*Patagioenas fasciata*)

Other Names: blue rock pigeon, band-tail

Name: American naturalist Thomas Say described and named this species in 1823 from specimens collected on Major Stephen Harriman Long's 1819–20 expedition to the Rocky Mountains and headwaters of the Missouri River. This bird was originally described as *Patagioenas fasciata* and was eventually shifted to the genus *Columba* (Latin for "dove"). However, due to genetic research, it has since been placed back into the genus *Patagioenas*. This genus name comes from combining the Latin word *patagium* (a gold edging or border) with the Greek word for wild pigeon, *oenas*. The specific name *fasciata* (band or banded) comes from the Latin word *fascia* (band, girdle, zone, strip, or stripe).

Description: Band-tailed pigeons are roughly the size of their domestic counterparts, averaging 12 ounces in weight. A male weighs nearly an ounce more than a female and has a slightly more rose-colored breast and a more vivid nape patch. Otherwise, the sexes are essentially identical. The band-tail is blue-gray, with slightly lighter undersides grading into a buff-colored vent. An iridescent patch of green feathers, bordered above by a narrow band of white, adorns the nape of the neck. The primary feathers are nearly black, and a diffuse dusky band crosses the tail near its midpoint. In a mature specimen, the black-tipped beak is yellow, as are the legs and feet. Eyelid rims are red. Young of the year tend to be lighter gray, lack the nape patch, and have paler feet and beak.

Only one of the two subspecies of band-tailed pigeon found in the United States occurs in Arizona: *Patagioenas fasciata fasciata*, the interior band-tailed pigeon.

Habitat and Range in Arizona: Band-tailed pigeons may be encountered in pine and pine-oak woodlands and in pinyon-juniper and chaparral habitats throughout Arizona. They are most abundant in the ponderosa pine forests along and below the Colorado Plateau from Flagstaff to the New Mexico border. Band-tails also frequent mixed live oak and pine woodlands of southern Arizona. Plants often associated  with band-tailed pigeon habitat include ponderosa pine, Apache pine, Chihuahuan pine, Gambel oak, Emory oak, silverleaf oak, netleaf oak, scrub oak, elderberry, and manzanita, among others.

Biology: Band-tailed pigeons in the United States are divided into two populations: the coastal population, which is found along the West Coast from southern Canada to northern Mexico; and the interior population, centered in the Rocky Mountains of the United States and Sierra Madre Mountains of Mexico. Band-tailed pigeons nest in Arizona and migrate south for the winter as fall approaches. The southeastern border of Arizona demarcates the northern reaches of this bird's wintering habitat.

Band-tailed pigeons begin returning from their wintering grounds in Durango and Sinaloa, Mexico, in March. They return to the places where they were born or nested the previous year. Band-tailed pigeons have a long breeding season, which extends from May through September. Male band-tails display to females with arching, stiff-winged glides similar to those performed by mourning doves. On the perch, the pair's courtship is accompanied by low, owl-like hoots or coos. The nest is constructed 18 feet or higher above the ground in the dense foliage of spruces, firs, pines, or oaks. One egg, rarely two, is laid in the flimsy nest doves and pigeons are well-known for making. Pairs may lay up to three clutches of eggs during the breeding season, but that is only under exceptional conditions. Eggs hatch after about 20 days of incubation. Both parents attend to the squabs. Special glands in the crop are developed by both parents. These glands secrete a nutritious substance known as "pigeon's milk," which sustains the quickly growing squab for the first few weeks of life. It takes roughly 50 days from the onset of courtship to fledging of young.

Acorns are a favorite food item and, when available, are utilized to the near exclusion of other food resources. Other dietary items include elderberries, mulberries, pinyon nuts and other pine seeds, agave seeds, agricultural grains, and various fruits and seeds.

Habits: Band-tailed pigeons prefer to perch in open, sparsely vegetated trees such as pine or oak snags. Often an individual will perch at or near the tree's highest point. Pigeons leave their roost and go to feed just after sunrise. Birds typically water after feeding. These birds frequent mineral springs and salt licks.

If acorns are scarce, band-tailed pigeons often migrate south early, vacating Arizona's northern and central mountain ranges in September. In the absence of acorns, use of elderberries and other mast crops increases. At these times, birds may concentrate in sites with an abundance of these fruits.

Like many birds, band-tailed pigeons spend midday resting in areas called "loafing sites." Loafing band-tailed pigeons tend to sit in open trees along ridgelines or other situations that command a view, from which they watch for predators. These loafing sites may be adjacent to a favored feeding area. The birds usually feed again in the afternoon before roosting for the night.

Band-tailed pigeons are powerful fliers and travel in flocks ranging from five to 40 birds. Their flight is direct, and routes often follow ridges or canyon edges. Pigeons are quiet when in flight, unless they pass close overhead, when their rushing wings can be heard. When startled, they leave the perch with a great clatter of wings.

Hunting Tips: How late these birds stay in Arizona in the fall depends largely on how good the acorn crop is. If the crop is poor, birds head south earlier. You will likely have your best luck locating band-tailed pigeons by finding areas with abundant acorns, and then searching for birds feeding or watering at nearby springs or ponds. Band-tailed pigeons will use alternative food sources such as pinyons and elderberries, especially in poor acorn years.

One way to hunt pigeons is to sit beneath a snag on a pine-country stock tank. Sitting quietly in the chill fall air on a high-country pond among changing leaves, listening to bugling elk, is one of the most enjoyable ways I can think of to spend a fall morning. Band-tails usually come to water early in the morning, after feeding, so check stock tanks early. If they are using the tank, they generally show up before 9 a.m. They also may be found feeding in dense stands of Gambel oak or other oak species. These birds like to loaf in pine snags and can

occasionally be found in these trees at midday along ridgetops. They may feed and water again in the late afternoon before roosting.

When searching for appropriate places to hunt, watch for band-tailed pigeons flying overhead or perched in trees. Binoculars can be particularly helpful for identifying sitting birds. Look for feathers or tracks along the water's edge, and for perched birds, to identify ponds being used by band-tails. Mineral springs, or stock ponds adjacent to canyons or salt licks, often are favored watering spots.

The most sporting way to take these birds is to locate their flight path and shoot them on the wing. The flight path may be a mountain saddle, ridgeline, or open approach to a stock tank. Their rapid, powerful flight makes for challenging shooting among the trees.

Gear: A game vest comes in handy for carrying ammunition and bagged birds to and from the vehicle. Shotguns of 28- to 12-gauge sizes are appropriate for taking band-tailed pigeons. Hunters find better success and fewer crippled birds when using one-ounce loads of No. 6 to 7½ shot for these tough birds. Open chokes such as improved cylinder or modified are most useful in taking flying birds. Camouflage is not necessary when hunting band-tailed pigeons, but dull-colored clothing blends in better if a stalk is required. Binoculars are helpful for spotting and identifying pigeons perched in treetops or flying across canyons. Hunters also find a warm sweater or coat a welcome addition while sitting in wait on cool, fall mornings.

Other Species: Band-tailed pigeons and tree squirrels are a natural combination, and it is not unusual for the hunter to encounter one while in search of the other. Abert's squirrels frequent many of the same habitats that band-tailed pigeons do. Though Nuttall's and eastern cottontails share some of these habitats as well, these rabbits are not commonly encountered in conifer woodlands.

Ducks, Geese, Swans: Anseriform Game Birds, Family Anatidae

These are chiefly aquatic birds with webbed feet and broad, flattened bills. A few species nest in the cavities or among the branches of trees, but the majority nest on the ground in dense vegetation near wetlands. With a few exceptions, birds in this group do not roost in trees, but rather rest on shorelines or sandbars, or sleep while afloat. Most are migratory. Ducks, geese, and swans are distributed worldwide, being absent only from Antarctica. Supraequatorial and subequatorial waterfowl faunas are fairly distinct, with little overlap. The United States is home to more than 40 species of ducks, geese, and swans. Due to the variety of species found in our state, ducks and geese will be addressed broadly in this publication rather than species by species.

Canada geese may be found wherever water is present.

Ring-necked duck.

Ducks

Some of the many species commonly encountered in Arizona are

- mallard *(Anas platyrhynchos)*
- northern pintail *(Anas acuta)*
- green-winged teal *(Anas crecca)*
- gadwall *(Anas strepera)*
- American wigeon *(Anas americana)*
- northern shoveler *(Anas clypeata)*
- ring-necked duck *(Aythya collaris)*
- bufflehead *(Bucephala albeola)*
- redhead *(Aythya americana)*
- canvasback *(Aythya valisineria)*

The common name for this waterfowl group, "duck," has its roots in Old English and is derived from the way many species plunge their head beneath the water when feeding. The Old English words *duce* and *ducan* mean "to dive and duck."

Description: The description varies depending on the species. In general, ducks have distinctly webbed feet and flattened bills. The body is stout. They possess powerful wings and are excellent fliers. Drakes (males) are usually more vividly colored than hens (females).

Habitat and Range in Arizona: Ducks are found in all appropriate habitats across the state. They may be encountered on almost any wetland habitat, including stock ponds, marshes, flooded areas, lakes, rivers, canals, etc.

Biology: Ducks are primarily winter migrants to and through Arizona, though a few members of some species nest and summer along our rivers, streams, and lakes. The majority of ducks found in the United States nest in central Canada southward to the northern United States. Several species begin their migrations early and pass through Arizona in late September and October, but we usually see our greatest influx of waterfowl in late November when winter storms force waterfowl down from northern states. Ducks are powerful fliers and may travel long distances to feed and roost. Mallards have been noted flying more than 20 miles to a food source. Flight speeds in excess of 60 miles per hour have been documented for some species.

Ducks are generally divided into two groups: divers and dabblers (puddle ducks). Diver ducks are those species that prefer deep water and dive to retrieve food items such as aquatic invertebrates, vertebrates, and vegetation. Diver ducks must run along the water's surface before gaining enough speed to take flight and typically sit low in the water, often with the tail resting flat on the water's surface. Dabblers, on the other hand, often feed on emergent or shallowly submerged plants (even agricultural crops) and can take flight with a single leap from the water's surface.

Pairing of some species occurs in the fall, and these ducks migrate and spend the winter as a pair until nesting commences. Nests for many species are well-concealed and constructed in close association with water, though some species of ducks, such as wigeons, seem to prefer drier nest sites away from water, and wood ducks and tree ducks (both rather uncommon in Arizona) nest in tree cavities. Nests are typically built of grass, reeds, leaves and other such items, and have a liberal lining of down and feathers. These nesting areas provide not only shelter but readily available feeding areas for the young and easy escape from terrestrial predators. A clutch of six eggs is typical for many species. For most ducks, the female is the sole attendant of the eggs, performing all incubation herself. The male usually abandons the female as soon as incubation commences. However, this is not true across the board, and both pintail and cinnamon teal drakes, among others, have been documented as staying near the nest and assisting with the rearing of young. The incubation period for many species is around 26 days.

Young are led to water, where they are safe from foxes and other land-based predators but suffer the predations of raptors, herons, turtles, fish, and other aquatic predators. Young ducks require a lot of protein and prey heavily on invertebrates for the first months of life. Mallards and many other species fledge in about two months and cannot fly before this time. By the fall, juvenile ducks look nearly identical to their mother. The adult male, having completed its molt just before migration, looks much like the hen, too.

Mortality for various waterfowl species can be fairly high. Mallards, for instance, suffer a mortality rate around 60% in the first two years of life. Life span varies considerably between duck species, but most routinely reach ages of three to six years. There are records of domestic mallards attaining age 25.

Habits: Ducks are most active in the first few hours of the day. They often start flying well before sunup and typically are situated in their feeding area before 9 a.m.

Male (below) and female mallard.

Ducks also move about on moonlit nights. Unsettled weather usually makes ducks move more frequently, and they tend to move more often and for longer periods on windy days. Ducks of all species tend to move immediately before the onset of inclement weather. Large winter fronts generally bring flights of ducks down from the north. Ducks will leave higher elevations in favor of warmer retreats where water has yet to freeze over.

Puddle ducks typically prefer water under 10 inches deep for feeding. Shallow flooded fields, river eddies, river backwaters, shallow coves of lakes, and stock ponds all are frequented by puddle ducks. Diver ducks frequent much deeper water and are more likely to be found on the deep runs and bends of rivers and on deep stock ponds and lakes.

A common problem experienced in Arizona, despite national nesting success, is warm winter weather. Often, warm winters in the western states "short-stop" many migrating waterfowl before they make it to the southern United States. So, while states north of Arizona (Utah, Nevada, etc.) enjoy fantastic hunting, we experience sporadic shooting at best. In the same manner, if warm weather keeps Arizona's high-country waters open, many ducks and geese spend the winter there rather than migrating to lower elevations. Simply put, many migrating waterfowl species go no farther south than they have to. If we have a warm winter, our state's high elevations are likely to offer the best hunting.

Hunting Tips: *Before you start hunting, check current regulations for changes from last year and current season dates and bag limits.* These guidelines are dynamic and based on breeding success and population numbers. They regularly change. The early part of the season offers the best opportunities for some early migrants, such as cinnamon and blue-winged teal. Mid- to late November is usually when waterfowl hunting in our low country picks up. By this time, free (unfrozen) water at northern latitudes typically becomes scarce, forcing birds southward to seek feeding and resting areas. Mornings after big winter storms and severe cold snaps are often an excellent time to check desert stock ponds for ducks.

Duck hunting with decoys can require a plethora of specialized items. Few other small-game pursuits boast such a formidable array of gadgets and gear for the hunter. Decoys will prove useful on lakes, rivers, and ponds. If you are decoying, start early. Have your decoys set and your blind built before legal shooting time comes. Set the decoys within easy shooting range of your blind.

A spread of decoys on a river backwater.

There are many popular formations employed by hunters when setting out decoys. Formations in a "U" or "J" shape are preferred by many. The hook of the "J" is placed in front of the blind. Some waterfowlers set their decoys out in lines, leading incoming ducks to the shooters. Others like to use open, amorphous sets, attempting to present a more natural appearance to ducks. In this instance, decoys should be set in a loose group, conveying the impression of a flock of relaxed, loafing or feeding birds. Leave a gap in the decoy spread where you want ducks to land. Most hunters prefer to place this gap near or in front of the blind. The gap should be 15 to 20 feet wide at least, making it easy for the ducks to find and land in. Most ducks land facing the wind (if it is substantial), so set your spread accordingly. Spinning-wing and other motion decoys are popular and work well. On occasion, motion decoys may cause experienced birds to flare. If birds are consistently flaring from your spread, try to figure out what is wrong and make adjustments. Keep in mind that no matter what you do, some birds will flare for no apparent reason: This is business as usual.

The blind for duck hunting does not need to be elaborate if you remain still when birds are approaching. Blinds should blend in well and can be constructed of materials found in the area. Carrying a pair of pruning shears in your decoy bag will allow you to clip some tamarisk, willow limbs, or other items to make a quick and effective blind. If at all possible, orient the blind so the sun is at your back. This helps when identifying waterfowl and of course keeps the sun out of your eyes. Often, it is possible to merely sit or kneel motionless among existing vegetation while waiting for birds to come in. Wearing camouflage helps you to blend into the surroundings, and employing a face mask allows you to watch incoming birds while minimizing the chance of being spotted. Avoid any quick movements while birds are working the decoys and try to watch them with a minimum of head movement.

Some considerations when decoying ducks:

- Don't place decoys too close together. This makes them look like frightened birds, which huddle together just before taking flight. Place decoys in loose groups, at random distances from each other. Try to convey a relaxed feeling with your spread.

- Avoid having decoys all face the same direction or setting them up in any other manner that gives them an unnatural appearance. Observe resting ducks in the wild and try to emulate that feel in your spread.

- Don't place the farthest decoys in your spread out of shooting range. Ducks often land outside the spread. By keeping your farthest decoys in range, you have a much greater chance of keeping short-stopping birds within gun range.

- Don't call too much, especially if you are a novice caller. Learn a few calls and use them to get the attention of passing or leaving birds. A general rule that works well for inexperienced callers is, if they are coming in, be quiet.

- Stay with the decoys. It is a near guarantee that if you leave the decoys because birds are landing elsewhere, birds will come in to the decoys. It is a great temptation to get out of the blind and move around when things are slow. Be patient. If you are caught out of the blind by incoming birds, freeze: Do not try to hide. Movement is much more likely to cause incoming waterfowl to flare than a motionless figure outside the blind.

Waterfowling coat, decoy, and calls.

- While moving about outside the blind, such as when retrieving fallen birds, keep a keen eye out for incoming ducks.

- Make yourself as comfortable as possible in your blind. Bring a small stool to sit on, or find a comfortable spot to kneel. The less movement taking place in the blind, the less chance ducks will spot you.

- Wear camouflage or drab clothing to help conceal yourself. A face mask will allow you to watch birds without letting them see your face shine in the light.

- Pick up all your spent shotshells and other items, such as food wrappers. Leave your hunting spot clean.

Once again, a little scouting is a big help in finding a productive hunting spot. Ducks tend to congregate in backwaters, slow runs on rivers, and sheltered areas on lakes, such as coves and the mouths of rivers and creeks. With some scouting, you will discover that though several spots look good and are used by ducks, they prefer one or a few spots. Typically, the best shooting is in the first couple hours of the day, so it is important to be ready by legal shooting time. Geese generally fly a little later than ducks, but you still want to be prepared by first light. To retrieve downed birds from stock tanks, try using a fishing rod rigged with a top-water plug. Cast over dead birds and reel them in. The same rig fitted with a diving plug will retrieve decoys in deep water by snagging the anchor line.

Tank Jumping: A very popular way to hunt ducks in Arizona is to "jump tanks" (visit water holes and shoot ducks flushed from them). This is a rather minimalist but very effective approach to an otherwise expensive and gear-laden sport. In some areas, many tanks can be visited in a short time, and if you plan a route, a day can easily be consumed driving from one pond to another. Many tanks can be viewed from a distant vantage point with binoculars to see if they hold waterfowl before you jump them. Caution must be taken not to scare the birds off the pond prematurely, so be quiet. Vehicles are best parked 50 to 100 yards from the intended target. Quietly approach the pond from the downstream side (below the dam, so you are out of sight). Pause at the base of the dam to ensure you and your party are organized, then rush to the top of the dam and be prepared to take any ducks scared off the water.

Gear: Most hunters find chest waders or hip boots useful when pursuing ducks. These come in a variety of configurations and materials. If you are likely to be hunting in brush or to have a long walk to your hunting area, consider waders made of abrasion- or tear-resistant materials. Camouflage clothing also is very helpful, and given the proclivity of waterfowl for inclement weather, waterproof material should be considered. Camouflage pattern is largely a matter of taste, but patterns with lots of browns blend effectively with winter landscapes. Also consider a head or face net to cover your face. These are handy and much more easily removed than face paints.

A dizzying array of duck decoys and calls are available to the enthusiast. For decoys, pick something you think looks good and presents a natural and relaxed posture. Teal decoys have the advantage of being small and easy to carry, and teal are widespread and common. One or two dozen decoys should be sufficient for most small bodies of water, but you may need more if you plan to hunt lakes or large rivers. Mixing some teal decoys with a handful of larger ones, such as mallards, can present a natural-looking setup.

A 16- to 12-gauge shotgun is ideal for waterfowl. The 20- or 28-gauge shotgun also can be used, but ammunition may be unduly expensive. Non-lead shot must be used for taking waterfowl in the United States, and currently a surfeit of choices are available. Due to the harsh environments generally encountered while waterfowl hunting, consider selecting a durable and reliable shotgun make. It is common for shotguns to be exposed to mud, water, brush, freezing temperatures, and dust, all on the same trip. For this reason, many hunters prefer inexpensive makes of firearms. Pump-action firearms tend to be more reliable than automatics under these conditions. If ducks will be taken at close range over decoys (15 to 20 yards), No. 6 steel shot generally works well. If longer shots are anticipated, No. 3 steel shot seems to be a good compromise. Numerous composite and non-lead types of shot are manufactured for waterfowlers. Many are heavier than lead and much heavier than steel and perform excellently. However, they also are typically much more expensive than steel.

When steel shot is in use, fowlers are likely to find open chokes more effective than unduly restricted ones such as full or extra-full. Steel shot is much harder than lead or many of the composite varieties of shot, and therefore does not deform when passing through a shotgun's choke. A tight choke employed with steel shot often causes an uneven shot pattern with many off-target pellets. Even with non-steel varieties of shot, when modern materials and ballistics are considered, chokes more restrictive than modified are likely to be of little value and in fact may compromise success.

Other Species: Snipe and geese are common cohabitants of many of the wetlands frequented by ducks. Ducks and geese can sometimes be successfully hunted at the same time by mixing decoys in areas where both are found. Along rivers, Gambel's quail, desert cottontail, eastern cottontail, and mourning dove may also be found.

Camouflage clothing is a big help when hunting waterfowl.

Canada goose.

Geese

Canada and snow geese are the species most commonly seen in Arizona. White-fronted and Ross's geese are also encountered occasionally.

Name: Both the Canada goose and snow goose were described by zoologist Carl Linnaeus in 1758. They belong to the genus *Branta*, which is Old Norse for "goose." The Canada goose's specific name, *canadensis*, means "from Canada." Though there is some debate about which genus the snow goose belongs to (formerly, it was in the genus *Anser*, which is Latin for "goose"), most taxonomists favor the genus *Chen*, which is Greek for "goose." The snow goose's specific name, *caerulescens*, means "sky blue" in Latin. The general name is derived from the Old English word for goose, *gos*.

Description: Geese are stout-bodied, short-legged waterfowl with long necks. Canada geese (*Branta canadensis*) weigh from three to 16 pounds and may have a wingspan in excess of four feet, depending on the race. Canada geese are buff brown with a white vent and dark rump, tail, and wings. The legs, bill, head, and neck are black. A large white patch is found on the cheek. Snow geese (*Chen caerulescens*) are white with pinkish feet and bills. The tips of the wings are black. They may weigh as much as six pounds. A dark phase of the snow goose, in which the bird has a dark-

Snow geese in flight.

colored body and a white head, also is commonly encountered. The body may have light mottling, and the neck may be white also. This form of the snow goose is often referred to as the "blue phase."

Habitat and Range in Arizona: Arizona is not renowned for its goose hunting. However, many of the refuges along the Colorado River are well-known goose-hunting areas. Geese may be encountered in nearly all habitats in Arizona if suitable water is present for feeding or loafing. Geese often are associated with larger bodies of water such as rivers or lakes, but they also stop off at small tanks and ponds to feed and rest. The Colorado, Salt, Gila, and Verde Rivers and associated lakes and other

areas house geese during winter. Some urban areas have well-established resident goose populations. These birds roost and nest on ponds such as those found on golf courses and feed on the greens or in nearby agricultural areas.

Biology: Geese generally are divided into two groups by wildlife management agencies. The term "light geese" refers to snow and Ross's geese, species that are typically light in color; while "dark geese" refers to Canada and white-fronted geese, species that are predominantly dark in color.

Many goose species are long-lived, exceeding 20 years. Some species are known to mate for life. This pairing behavior may not be as absolute as once thought, and some current research indicates that geese and many other birds switch partners more often than once believed. Geese do show great fidelity to their birth and nesting areas.

Canada geese typically nest in emergent flora such as cattails or reeds. Islands are favored nesting sites. They lay an average of five eggs and, as with other geese, both parents attend to the young. Eggs hatch roughly 30 days after incubation begins. Young can fly in two to three months.

Snow geese nest on the open tundra of Alaska. Nesting typically begins at the end of May or in early June. Three to five white eggs are laid and hatch in about 22 days. Goslings mature rapidly, reaching nearly adult size by the time of migration in fall. In recent decades, snow-goose numbers have increased dramatically, and biologists are concerned the birds may be damaging fragile nesting habitats. In response, hunting seasons for this species have been prolonged and bag limits liberalized in an effort to control their population.

Geese tend to live longer than ducks. On average, most geese live about five to seven years, but many have the potential to live much longer. One banded Canada goose lived to age 33.

Habits: Geese tend to move later and longer than most other waterfowl species. It is not unusual to see geese flying at any time of day. Geese generally head to their roost at dusk, though they may spend midday loafing on the roost if it is close to where they feed. They typically travel in flocks, which may be quite large (numbering several hundred birds) depending on the species. These large birds leave the roost after daylight, when they fly out to feeding areas. Geese favor green feed, and foraging sites may be agricultural fields, backwaters and main channels of rivers and creeks, or desert mesas or flats covered with succulent winter forbs. Geese are creatures of habit and tend to follow a daily routine. This routine is generally adhered to until some interruption prompts a change of behavior. Interruptions may take on many forms, such as a change of weather, disturbance at the feeding site, or depletion of food resources. Geese can be quite vocal both on the ground and in the air.

Hunting Tips: Geese may be taken by a variety of methods; the two most popular are jump-shooting and decoying.

Jump-shooting can be done over water or fields. As when jump-shooting ducks, typically you spot birds ahead of time, often with the use of binoculars. Plan a stalk; when in range, stand and shoot birds. Geese are very wary and notoriously difficult to approach. Avoiding 15 or more pairs of nervous eyes is a difficult task for any predator.

As for decoying, there is an old saying, "It takes two days to kill a goose." This is largely true. Decoying geese requires scouting and patterning. Determine a flock's daily routine, then exploit their behavior to your advantage. Typically, you should position yourself in a vantage point where undisturbed geese can be observed. Note flyways and foraging locations. Scout these locations to determine the exact position of birds. It is important not to disturb geese during this process. Birds should be allowed to leave their feeding site of their own accord. After the geese have left, determine exactly where the geese were feeding by looking for feathers and fresh droppings. Ideally, place decoys at or near the spot where goose sign is found and erect a discreet blind within gun range.

Camouflage is helpful in keeping you concealed. Remaining motionless while birds are working the area is very important. If you wish to watch birds work the decoys, a camouflage face mask is an essential clothing item. But even when using a face mask, keep movements to a minimum: Birds are best watched with your face down, from the corners of your eyes, and from behind a screen of brush. It is better if other hunters in the blind keep their faces down and remain motionless until the one watching the geese calls the shot.

Geese often respond well to calling, decoys, and flagging. They tend to shy away from tall cover such as uncut fields or heavy brush along field edges. Keep this in mind when setting decoys. Decoys should be set in a loose, relaxed flock, not huddled close together, with the exception of a couple of groups of two or three decoys meant to represent family groups. Watch undisturbed feeding and resting geese and try to emulate the way they looked when setting out decoys. Also notice that geese generally face into the wind when feeding. Keep this in mind when setting decoys. Use several types of decoys, such as windsock styles that turn with the wind and add movement to your decoy spread. Place the farthest decoys in the spread within gun range. A "V" or sickle pattern for the decoy spread often works well and is preferred by many hunters. The bottom of the "V" should be closest to the blind.

Commercial blinds work well and are a matter of preference. In some situations,

such as when hunting the middle of an open field, hunters may find a layout-style blind to be the best option. However, blinds often can be constructed of local vegetation by modifying some existing feature such as a ditch, fencerow, or field edge.

Stay with decoys even when hunting is slow: Geese have an uncanny habit of showing up as soon as you leave the decoy spread. Often, geese come in silently and catch the snoozing shooter unaware. Remaining in the field until after the evening flight ends (when birds have returned to the roost for the night) is a good strategy for the serious goose hunter.

Gear: Jump-shooting requires much less investment in gear than decoying. A good pair of binoculars is useful in spotting birds on distant ponds and fields. Field glasses are also helpful when scouting for places to hunt or for patterning birds.

Handy items for hunting geese:

- Various kinds of camouflage clothing and face masks are available for cold-weather hunting and will be appreciated when you are lying in a field on a January morning.

- Many types of goose calls are available. Find one that is easy for you to use, and learn a few simple calls to help distant geese spot your decoys.

- Flags for both dark and light geese can be had through many sporting-goods outlets. These are employed when geese are too far away to spot the hunter who is waving to them. Flags simulate a goose landing or stretching its wings. Use flags in conjunction with calls to draw the attention of passing geese to your decoys.

- Because geese often are shot over fields, waders are not usually required.

Goose decoys come in almost as many varieties as goose calls. Selecting decoys can be overwhelming. Many things should be considered before making a substantial investment, such as: Will you be hunting over fields or water? Can you drive right up to your hunting spot, or will you have to carry decoys a long way? Do you have a friend with a weak mind and strong back who is willing to share the load? Several companies make ultra-realistic full-body decoys that have proven their effectiveness on many a hunt. If you wish to hunt a place where decoys must be carried in for a great distance, you will find shell or silhouette-type decoys more manageable than bulkier varieties. The number of decoys used is mainly a matter of preference and of what can be carried into the field. Where geese don't get much hunting pressure, a dozen or fewer often works well. If you choose to hunt one of the wildlife refuges or

Snow geese often congregate in large flocks.

other places where geese are regularly shot, you are likely to find a few dozen decoys or more will serve better. Additionally, snow geese tend to travel in larger flocks and typically respond better to larger decoy spreads. For pursuing light geese, you may need to invest in several dozen decoys. If this is the case, you will find rag-style decoys may be your least expensive option.

A 12-gauge shotgun is ideal for these large birds. Hunters may also wish to consider 10- and 16-gauge shotguns, which are both effective gauges

for waterfowl hunting, but ammunition can be very expensive for these guns. Waterfowl hunting often has the disadvantage of punishing firearms with abundant moisture, mud, freezing conditions, and all manner of debris. The best choice for waterfowl of all sorts is a durable and reliable shotgun make, something not too expensive that works under the most adverse conditions. Smaller gauges should mostly be avoided, unless shots are close and carefully chosen and heavy shot sizes are used. It is important to minimize the potential of crippling birds. In addition, ammunition for these smaller gauges is often cost-prohibitive. Three-inch magnum shells are useful, but 2¾-inch magnum cartridges work just fine under most conditions.

Non-lead ammunition is required for taking waterfowl. Steel shot is a popular alternative, but has poorer downrange energy than do some of the heavier non-lead varieties. Steel shot sizes employed for geese should be large, preferably BB or some similar size. Larger shot sizes, up to a point, provide greater knockdown power for body-shot birds. If you are using one of the excellent and numerous heavier-than-lead varieties of shot on the market, No. 2 shot is a good choice. These types of shotshells can be very expensive but often are worth the investment, due to their excellent performance. Avoid F, T, and TTT-sized shot, as research has shown them to be less effective than the smaller sizes and more likely to cripple birds.

A lot has been written about steel shot and shotgun chokes. Because steel shot is harder than lead, it does not deform when passing through a tightly constricted choke, which can cause everything from erratic shot patterns to bulged barrels in guns not approved for use with such chokes. You will have better results if you use chokes no tighter than modified when using steel shot. And considering modern ballistics and shotshell components, this advice holds true for all types of shotshells unless you are taking very long shots.

Other Species: Ducks of various species often use the same bodies of water for roosting and feeding that geese do. Marshlands and rivers may also hold snipe. Gambel's quail, cottontails, and mourning doves are attracted to rivers and wetlands not only for the water but also for the cover and food resources they provide.

Small Game Mammals

Introduction to Squirrel and Rabbit Hunting

Arizona is home to several species of small game mammals and offers year-round hunting opportunities. Cottontail rabbits and tree squirrels are the only mammals currently classified by the Arizona Game and Fish Department as small game mammals. However, jackrabbits and several other small mammals are open to take with the purchase of a hunting license.

Desert cottontail.

Three species of cottontail and four species of tree squirrel are available to the Arizona hunter. Cottontails may be hunted all year, while tree squirrels can be taken only during a fall season, for the most part. Jackrabbits have a year-round season.

Small game mammals and jackrabbits are generally hunted by walking through appropriate habitat. They are an underexploited resource in Arizona and offer an excuse to visit some remote and beautiful country, as well as a reason to be afield even if that precious elk or deer tag was not drawn. Unlike hunting some of the small game birds, pursuing small game mammals requires minimal equipment. A day outdoors can be enjoyed with little more than field clothes, a favorite firearm, and a good pair of walking shoes.

Tree Squirrels, Family Sciuridae

Arizona gray squirrel.

Most people would be surprised to learn Arizona has more different species of tree squirrel than any other state in the United States. Four species of two different genera inhabit our woodlands: Abert's, Arizona gray, Apache fox, and red. Though some biologists consider Arizona gray squirrels and Apache fox squirrels the same species, there is good evidence they are distinct, so they are treated as such in this publication. Despite originally being considered a distinct species, the well-known Kaibab squirrel is a subspecies of the Abert's squirrel that is confined to habitats north of the Grand Canyon. Three of our squirrels are considered large species and reach sizes in the range of two pounds. Red squirrels, the exception, seldom reach one pound.

Tree squirrels are rodents and, like other rodents, have large incisors that grow throughout the animal's life. Growth of these teeth is kept in check by constant use. Arizona tree squirrels use their incisors for stripping bark from trees, peeling conifer cones, and clipping vegetation. Like most small mammals, tree squirrels have numerous predators. Some raptors such as goshawks are squirrel specialists, and mammals such as foxes are known squirrel predators as well. Squirrels also fall prey to snakes: The gopher snake is one species that has been documented taking both young and adult squirrels. One road-killed six-foot-long gopher snake found below the Mogollon Rim had four juvenile Arizona gray squirrels in its stomach.

All of Arizona's tree squirrels prefer habitats with mature trees that are tall and have interlocking crowns. These habitats allow squirrels to travel and forage without exposing themselves to terrestrial dangers. Large trees not only allow safe travel but also offer nesting sites. Nests may be situated near the ends of limbs and are constructed of materials such as leaves, conifer needles, bark, and grasses. Some nests are built in tree cavities.

Occasionally, more than one species of squirrel can be found in the same or adjacent habitat. In many areas in central Arizona, Arizona gray squirrels and Abert's squirrels can be found together where pine woodlands interface with riparian corridors. However, all of Arizona's tree squirrels are essentially solitary. They congregate only for breeding and occasionally when abundant localized food sources bring animals together.

The genus name for these species, *Sciurus*, is derived from the Greek word *skiouros*, which means "squirrel" or literally "shadow tail" (*skia* means "shadow," and *oura* means "tail"). The name was given by the forefather of modern classification, Carl Linnaeus, in 1758.

Abert's Squirrel *(Sciurus aberti)*

Other Names: tassel-eared squirrel, Abert's tree squirrel, Kaibab squirrel, tree squirrel

Name: Dr. S. W. Woodhouse, a naturalist, is responsible for describing this species from specimens collected in 1853 in the San Francisco Peaks area near Flagstaff. This squirrel was originally dubbed *Sciurus dorsalis*, but this name had been given previously to another species. Woodhouse quickly renamed the squirrel after Colonel J. W. Abert, a topographic engineer. Three subspecies occur in Arizona: *S. a. aberti, S. a. chuscensis*, and *S. a. kaibabensis*. Both *chuscensis* and *kaibabensis* refer to places the squirrels inhabit; in this case, the Chuska Mountains and Kaibab Plateau, respectively.

Description: Abert's squirrels are large, arboreal squirrels weighing from one to (rarely) just over two pounds. The Kaibab squirrel subspecies, *S. a. kaibabensis*, is separated from the others by the Grand Canyon. This subspecies originally was thought to be a separate species. The Kaibab squirrel is easily differentiated from the others by its black ventral color, all-white tail, and obscure eye ring. Occasionally, an Abert's squirrel with dark undersides is encountered south of the Colorado River, or an Abert's squirrel with light undersides is found north of the Colorado River. The Abert's squirrel is dark gray dorsally, typically with a rusty-red stripe running down the center of the back. The tail is long, densely haired, and gray on top. Specimens south of the Colorado River are white on the belly and the underside of the tail and have a distinct white eye ring. A narrow black stripe extends between the forelimbs and hind limbs, separating the dark dorsum from the light underside. All Abert's squirrels sport long ear tassels in winter.

Habitat and Distribution in Arizona: Abert's squirrels are creatures of pine forests. They typically are associated with ponderosa pine but, due to transplants, may now be found in other pine woodland habitats. Before transplant efforts, this squirrel was found in ponderosa pine forests along the Colorado Plateau, on the south and north rims of the Grand Canyon, and in the Chuska Mountain area.
It has been introduced into the Bradshaw, Santa Catalina, Hualapai, Pinal, Pinaleño, and Granite Mountains; the Hualapai Reservation; and Mount Logan. After these introductions, Abert's squirrels spread to the Superstition, Rincon, Sawmill, and Mazatzal Mountains and to Mounts Ord, Trumbull, and Emma. The ponderosa pine is the plant species most often associated with Abert's squirrels. Gambel oak, maple, sycamore, ash, pinyon, and juniper may also be present but are less important.

Biology: Abert's squirrels feed primarily on the cones, seeds, inner bark, buds, and flowers of the ponderosa pine tree. Another important food source is fungi associated with pine trees, which these squirrels dig up and consume. Acorns, shrubs, grasses, mistletoe, insects, carrion, shed antlers, and bones also have been documented in the diet of these squirrels. Abert's squirrels do not store food to any great extent and must remain active throughout the winter. Persistent deep snow has a deleterious effect on squirrels, limiting their diet to the less nutritious inner bark (phloem) of conifers. This resource is accessed by clipping the terminal clump of needles from branches. The bark is stripped and the phloem eaten. If forced to subsist on this diet for a couple of months, Abert's squirrels lose weight and suffer increased mortality. Free water is not required for the existence of these animals, though it is readily taken when available.

Nests of pine needles, grasses, and occasionally leaves are built among the limbs of pine trees. A single squirrel usually constructs many nests within its home range.

Of the squirrels found in Arizona, only Abert's sport ear tassels.

Nests are used for taking shelter in poor weather, sleeping, and rearing young. Mating typically occurs in April and May, and a female remains in estrus for less than a day. Not all females reproduce each year. Receptive females are followed by many males and may mate with several. Two to five young are born in June or July. Young emerge from the nest in August and are weaned by mid- to late September.

Abert's squirrels can reach astonishing densities when environmental conditions permit. More than 100 squirrels per square mile have been recorded during these periods. Uncut forests have been documented as harboring the greatest number of Abert's squirrels, with populations being as much as five times higher than in surrounding areas. Typically, Abert's squirrels can be found at densities of 15–30 animals per square mile.

Habits: Abert's squirrels prefer forest habitats featuring ponderosa pine trees 15 feet or taller with interlocking crowns. Squirrels may travel from tree to tree for great distances. Abert's squirrels often forage on the ground, and it is not unusual to find them running across the forest floor. Threatened squirrels quickly take to the trees, often climbing to the highest point or the end of a branch, where they conceal themselves in a clump of needles. Frightened squirrels also may flatten

The dark belly and all-white tail distinguish Kaibab squirrels from other Abert's. All Abert's squirrels typically lose their ear tassels in the summer.

themselves against the upper sides of branches and remain motionless for long periods of time. Abert's squirrels can be encountered at any time of day but are most active in the morning and least active in late afternoon. These squirrels can be wide-ranging. Home ranges of up to 18 acres have been recorded. Squirrels are less active in inclement weather, and when it is cold, they may bask in the sun before becoming active.

Nests typically are found from 16–90 feet up in ponderosa pines and are situated in a fork formed by a branch and the tree trunk. Nests often are located on the south side of the tree, presumably for warmth. Nests are occasionally located in the cavities of trees such as oaks or cottonwoods. Nest numbers are a general indication of local squirrel abundance.

Hunting Tips: Start your search for Abert's squirrels early, especially in sunny or warm weather when squirrels are most active. Be in the field as soon after sunrise as possible. Watch for squirrel sign beneath ponderosa pines, such as stripped cones and clipped terminal pine-needle clusters. Walk quietly along logging roads and search for squirrels foraging on the ground and in trees. When a squirrel is spotted on the ground, it may be shot on the ground or rushed and chased up a tree (dogs can prove useful in this last activity). Chasing squirrels up trees at 7,000 feet elevation is a lot more work than it sounds, especially uphill.

The classic way to hunt squirrels is to walk quietly into likely looking habitat and take a seat beneath a tree. It is important to keep noise and movements to a minimum. Wait until squirrels begin to move again. This may take more than 30 minutes, but typically squirrels resume activity in 10–15 minutes. Use your eyes and ears to locate squirrels. Watch for the silhouette of squirrels among the branches of trees, and for movements such as waving pine branches as squirrels jump from tree to tree. Listen for the sound of falling cones or needle clusters, barking squirrels, squirrels chewing on cones or climbing trees, or other noises or movements that may betray the presence of a squirrel.

Gear: Binoculars are particularly helpful in spotting motionless squirrels in the tops of trees. These rodents often seem to vanish once they stop moving. Shotguns work well for squirrels, and smaller gauges are quite adequate: 20-gauge, 28-gauge, and .410-bore shotguns shooting shot sizes of No. 7½ to 6 are perfect for penetrating the morass of small limbs and pine needles in which squirrels typically hide. If you wish to avoid the problem of picking shot from your meal and want to increase the sport of pursuing these animals, consider using a .22-caliber rifle or, if you are really brave, a .22-caliber pistol. This is the most sporting way to take squirrels, and affords the opportunity to place shots to minimize damage to the meat. Open sights often prove difficult to use on small targets in the low light of forests and at the extreme shooting angles offered by squirrels. A scope saves ammunition in the long run and improves success.

Archery equipment can also be used for squirrels, but they are difficult targets. Use blunt-tipped arrows to improve the odds of retrieving the arrow after it is shot.

Camouflage clothing is not necessary, but some sort of drab or dark shirt and pants will prove useful. Otherwise, you need comfortable, durable shoes and clothing appropriate for the weather. Remember, you may need to sit still for long periods, and it is easy to get cold when you're not moving. A game vest comes in handy to carry bagged squirrels if you plan on taking a long walk or moving far from your vehicle.

Other Species: Band-tailed pigeons are common in the ponderosa pine forests where most Abert's squirrels are found. They frequent many of the same places, including stock tanks and dense stands of pine. Where ponderosa pine is found next to riparian vegetation or spruce-fir forest, Abert's squirrels may be found with Arizona gray and red squirrels, respectively. Black-tailed jackrabbits are uncommon residents in Abert's squirrel habitat. Though Abert's squirrels prefer lower-elevation habitats, they can occasionally be found together with dusky grouse.

Arizona Gray Squirrel *(Sciurus arizonensis)*

Other Names: gray squirrel, tree squirrel, Huachuca gray squirrel, Catalina gray squirrel, fox squirrel

Name: Naturalist C. Elliot Coues named this species in 1867 from specimens collected in the Bradshaw Mountains at or near Fort Whipple. The species name *arizonensis* means "from Arizona" and is given for the state in which the type specimen was collected. Though there is some debate among biologists, currently three subspecies of Arizona gray squirrels are recognized: *S. a. arizonensis*, *S. a. catalinae*, and *S. a. huachuca*. These subspecific names are derived from the places they inhabit; in this case, Arizona, the Catalina Mountains, and the Huachuca Mountains, respectively. Further taxonomic debates surround this species. Some biologists believe the Arizona gray squirrel and Chiricahua fox squirrel are the same species or are subspecies of the closely related eastern fox squirrel, *Sciurus niger*.

Description: This large, arboreal, gray-colored squirrel has rounded ears (no ear tufts), a white eye ring, a long and bushy tail, and a white belly. The dark, grizzled tail is bordered by white. The Arizona gray squirrel ranges in weight from just over a pound to just under two pounds and reaches about 20 inches in length. It often has a rufous wash to the dorsum and top of tail. The dorsal salt-and-pepper gray can range from dark to silver. During the warm months, when Abert's squirrels lack ear tassels, they can be easily mistaken for this species. However, gray squirrels lack the black stripe between the dark upper parts and white underparts.

Habitat and Range in Arizona: Gray squirrels inhabit drainages and mountains just below the Mogollon Rim. They also are found in the Bradshaw, Pine, Santa Catalina, Rincon, Santa Rita, Huachuca, Patagonia, Pajarito, and Atascosa Mountains.

Gray squirrels are primarily a riparian species. They prefer creek bottoms and moist canyons where tall, deciduous, riparian trees with interlocking crowns provide food and shelter. Tree species often associated with Arizona gray squirrels are sycamore, Fremont cottonwood, Arizona walnut, velvet ash, boxelder, bigtooth maple, Gambel oak, evergreen oaks, ponderosa pine, Arizona cypress, and willows. Riparian corridors adjacent to pine woodlands are optimal habitat in central Arizona. In southern Arizona, gray squirrels frequent canyons that drain "sky island" mountain ranges. Plants associated with these areas include Arizona madrone, Chihuahuan pine, and Apache pine, along with many of the aforementioned tree species.

Biology: Arizona gray squirrels are in fact fox squirrels and share many characteristics, such as dentition and skull measurements, with others of their kind. Like Abert's squirrels, Arizona gray squirrels do not cache food to any significant degree and remain active year-round. Mast crops such as acorns, walnuts, juniper berries, pine seeds, and hackberries comprise the bulk of their diet. Various sorts of fungi also are important foods, as are flowers and buds of riparian trees and plants.

Peak breeding months for Arizona gray squirrels are April and May, but they may start as early as January. Breeding coincides with the flowering of riparian tree species. Similar to Abert's squirrels, gray squirrels engage in breeding chases where several amorous males may pursue a receptive female. Two to four young are born from January through October. However, young are most commonly born in May and June. Research indicates that females produce only one litter a year, and not all females breed each year.

Nests are similar to those of the Abert's squirrel and are constructed of leaves, grasses, twigs, shredded bark, and other items. This squirrel builds multiple nests within its home range and uses these shelters as needed. Nests serve as nighttime shelters, places to rear young, and retreats from the elements.

Arizona gray squirrels are decidedly less common than Abert's squirrels. The limited extent of primary habitat (riparian corridors) available to this species prohibits population densities on the magnitude of those seen with Abert's squirrels.

Habits: This species prefers mature trees 75 feet or more in height, though it may be encountered in smaller trees. Gray squirrels are most active in the morning, but remain active much of the day. On occasion, more than one squirrel may be found feeding in the same tree.

When disturbed, these squirrels may freeze for several minutes or longer. One frightened squirrel was observed to lie motionless on a limb for more than an hour. To avoid predators, gray squirrels flatten themselves against tree trunks or limbs, making them very difficult to see. It is not uncommon for a harassed squirrel to run rapidly through the treetops for a great distance. The agility displayed at these times is awe-inspiring. This species conceals itself less often in the terminal clumps of pine needles than do Abert's squirrels. Gray squirrels also are quieter than Abert's. Though their calls sound similar, gray squirrels vocalize less frequently and with reduced fervor.

Gray squirrels may be found on the ground, foraging for fungi and other items or collecting nest materials. While on the ground, they frequently freeze for a moment or two before moving again. Occasionally, gray squirrels may be encountered away from river bottoms. If the riparian habitat is of sufficient quality, gray squirrels may follow these corridors into desert habitats.

Hunting Tips: Wandering around in the beauty of fall creek bottoms among the gold, red, and yellow of changing and falling leaves is reason enough to pursue this challenging species. Start looking for gray squirrels early in the morning. Move quietly along the edges of riparian corridors, keeping an eye out for squirrels. Watch the trees and ground inside the riparian area and adjacent woodlands for squirrels and movement. Search for shredded cones, shelled acorns, nests, squirrel tracks in mud, and other signs that betray the presence of squirrels.

Walk quietly into likely looking habitat and take a seat beneath a tree. Sit where you can command a good view of many trees and as much riparian bottomland as possible. It is important to keep noise and movements to a minimum, as squirrels

are wary and easily disturbed. Wait until squirrels begin to move again, and then pursue accordingly. This may take more than 30 minutes, but typically squirrels resume activity within several minutes of being disturbed. Listen for the sounds of foraging and moving squirrels, such as falling leaves or cones, barking squirrels, squirrels chewing on cones, and the scratching sound of squirrel claws on tree bark. Also, carefully scan trees for the silhouette of motionless squirrels and for movements such as waving branches as squirrels jump from tree to tree.

Once a squirrel is sighted, move yourself into shooting position. Keep an eye on the squirrel, especially if it is moving. It is easy to lose sight of your quarry in the dense vegetation of riparian areas. It is not unusual, while sitting quietly, to spot more than one squirrel at a time. A partner will prove useful in keeping track of quarry, especially when multiple squirrels are concerned.

Gear: The same gear used when hunting other tree-squirrel species is needed when hunting gray squirrels. Binoculars are particularly useful for spotting squirrels in trees. Too often, an unidentifiable dark mass is sighted in a tree, and only a good pair of binoculars allows proper identification. A few types of firearms are particularly well-suited for squirrel hunting. Shotguns are favored by many, and work well for squirrels. The smaller gauges (20-gauge, 28-gauge, and .410-bore) are quite adequate. Shotguns shooting shot sizes of No. 7½ to 6 are perfect for penetrating the often dense screen of pine needles and small branches that typically obscure shots at squirrels. However, there is nothing more effective and sporting than to use a scoped .22-caliber rifle. Aside from possibly a .22-caliber pistol or bow, this is the most sporting way to take squirrels, and .22-caliber rifles afford the opportunity to place shots that minimize damage to the meat. Open sights can also be employed, but dim light, small target size, and difficult angles often conspire against the shooter. A scope definitely saves ammunition and frustration in the long run. Though camouflage clothing is not required, drab clothing is helpful. Otherwise, choose a good pair of field shoes, especially if you plan on hiking, and some warm clothing to keep the winter chill off. If you plan on still-hunting, you will appreciate warm clothing.

Other Species: Band-tailed pigeons sometimes loaf, feed, and water in the canyon riparian corridors and adjacent bluffs used by gray squirrels. In the oak woodlands of southern Arizona, band-tailed pigeons and Arizona gray squirrels can be found using the same habitats. Abert's squirrels occur sympatrically where riparian corridors slice through ponderosa pine habitats.

Chiricahua Fox Squirrel *(Sciurus nayaritensis)*

Other Names: Apache squirrel, Apache fox squirrel, Mexican fox squirrel, Nayarit squirrel, fox squirrel

Name: The taxonomy of this squirrel is a confusing story, muddled by the sometimes variable appearance of this species. The first specimen of *Sciurus nayaritensis* was collected in 1890 on an expedition to Zacatecas, Mexico, in the Sierra de Valparaiso. It was described by zoologist Joel Asaph Allen that same year as *Sciurus alstoni*. However, Allen quickly learned the specific name was already in use and renamed the squirrel *S. nayaritensis*, for the Nayarit Mountains of the Sierra Madres. In 1893, Allen described another specimen of this same squirrel, taken on an expedition to northern Sonora and Chihuahua, as *Sciurus apache*, in honor of the early Native American peoples who inhabited those mountains. Shortly afterward, the first specimen in the United States was collected in Cave Creek Canyon, in the Chiricahua Mountains of southeastern Arizona. It was described as *Sciurus chiricahuae* by E. A. Goldman in 1933. Eventually, all these specimens were recognized as representing a single species and combined under the name *Sciurus nayaritensis*. One subspecies of this squirrel occurs in Arizona: *S. n. chiricahuae*, named for the mountain range where it is found.

Description: This is a large arboreal squirrel with grizzled gray or brown upper parts infused with rusty orange (ochre). It possesses ochre sides, underparts, and feet. The tail is long and thickly haired, dark gray to black above and rusty orange below, bordered by lighter tan or yellow hair. A ring of ocherous hair surrounds the eye and an orange patch is located behind each ear. Occasionally, this orange color extends onto the lower back in the area above the tail. This species averages about a pound and a half in weight (25 ounces), but exceptional specimens may approach two pounds. Lengths average 21 inches, about half of which is tail.

Habitat and Range in Arizona: This species primarily inhabits canyon bottoms. It typically lives in deciduous broad-leafed riparian corridors and adjacent pine-oak woodlands. In the United States, it is found only in the Chiricahua Mountains of southeastern Arizona. Plants often associated with this species include Apache and Chihuahuan pine, madrone, Arizona cypress, sycamore, and live oaks.

Biology: The Apache fox squirrel resembles the Arizona gray squirrel in form, habits, and biology. This species is most commonly encountered at elevations between 5,500 and 6,500 feet and typically is associated with riparian areas.

Seeds make up the bulk of this squirrel's diet: 96% of the summer diet and 77% of the winter diet are various seeds. Fungi are also used extensively, especially in cooler months. Winter diets are largely composed of the fruit of Arizona cypress and mistletoe. Other food items utilized by this squirrel are acorns of Arizona white, Emory, and silverleaf oaks; manzanita berries; Arizona walnuts; and the seeds of Apache pine, Chihuahuan pine, Douglas-fir, alligator juniper, sycamore, Arizona madrone, and Fremont cottonwood.

Chiricahua fox squirrels have the lowest known reproductive rate among North American squirrels. An average of one young is born per year. Rarely, this squirrel may produce a litter with two or three young. Fox squirrels begin nesting as early as April. Emergence of the young occurs from May through August. Due to low reproduction rates and large home ranges, population densities of Chiricahua fox squirrels are very low when compared to those of other North American squirrel species. They are not common in any of the habitats where they occur in Arizona.

Nests called "dreys" are constructed of leaves, pine needles, shredded bark, grasses, and other debris. Chiricahua fox squirrels build multiple nests in areas they frequent. Nests may be constructed in tree cavities but often are built on tree limbs, typically toward the tip. Nests are used for sheltering and rearing young. Oaks and pines are favored trees for nesting.

As with many species of mammal, male Chiricahua fox squirrels are more wide-ranging than their female counterparts. Males move more frequently and over longer distances during their early-season breeding period. These home ranges show little seasonal variation in both sexes.

Habits: Fox squirrels are most active during the morning and afternoon during summer months. In the winter, they are active throughout the day. When disturbed, they often remain motionless for long periods, sometimes in plain sight. Their typical response to being frightened when in the open is to flee to the nearest large tree, where they shelter behind the trunk or retreat into a cavity. They are said to be less agile than other tree squirrels and have been observed to slip or slide often while climbing the trunks of trees.

They spend a good deal of time foraging on the ground and sometimes aggregate in areas with abundant resources. These squirrels are mostly silent, but do produce raspy, barking alarm calls when agitated.

Hunting Tips: Due to this squirrel's limited distribution, low reproductive potential, and scant numbers, hunters should approach the harvest of this species conservatively. Though they are, like other squirrels, excellent to eat, the Chiricahua fox squirrel should be collected more as a specimen for its uniqueness than as an item for the table. Sportspeople are encouraged to limit their take and act as responsible conservationists.

Hunting the Chiricahua fox squirrel is much like pursuing the Arizona gray squirrel. Concentrate efforts along creek bottoms with diverse assemblages of riparian trees such as sycamore, cypress, and walnut, with adjacent hillsides of Apache and Chihuahuan pine, alligator juniper, manzanita, and live oaks. Watch for the silhouette of motionless squirrels in trees. Search for signs of squirrel activity such as shredded cones, digging, nests in trees, tracks, and clipped pine branch-tips. Move quietly into the area to be hunted and find a place to sit quietly. Remain as motionless as possible, to keep any disturbances to a minimum. Choose a site from which the most country can be viewed.

Wait until squirrels begin to move again. This may take quite some time, maybe more than 30 minutes. Often, squirrels resume activity in 10–15 minutes. However, Chiricahua fox squirrels are notorious for remaining motionless. Listen for the sound of rustling leaves, the sound of squirrels scuttling on trees, barking squirrels, squirrels chewing on cones, and other noises or movements that betray the presence of a squirrel. Watch for movement such as waving branches as squirrels jump from tree to tree. Once a squirrel is sighted, move into a position from which a clear shot can be taken. Keep an eye on the squirrel, as they quickly disappear among the dense vegetation of riparian areas.

Gear: Gear is the same as for pursuing other squirrels. Binoculars are particularly helpful in spotting squirrels in the tops of trees. Shotguns work well for squirrels, and the smaller gauges (20-gauge, 28-gauge, and .410-bore) are quite adequate for these small mammals. Shotguns shooting shot sizes of No. 7½ to 6 are best for punching through the needles and limbs where squirrels often conceal themselves. If you are looking for a more sporting way to take squirrels, consider a scoped .22-caliber rifle. This method also affords the opportunity to place shots to minimize damage to the meat. If you are collecting the squirrel for a mount, a shotgun or .22 shot to the chest will best preserve the quality of your specimen. Open sights often prove difficult to use on squirrels. These are small targets, and lighting is often poor in woodlands. A scope saves ammunition in the long run. Camouflage clothing is not necessary, but a drab or dark shirt and pants may prove useful. Otherwise, you need comfortable, durable shoes and clothing appropriate for the weather. Remember, you may need to sit still for long periods, and it is easy to get cold when you're not moving.

Other Species: The southeastern riparian corridors most often used by this species are also frequented by band-tailed pigeons.

Red Squirrel *(Tamiasciurus hudsonicus)*

Other Names: North American red squirrel, spruce squirrel, chickaree, pine squirrel

Name: The red squirrel was named by German naturalist Johann Christian Polycarp Erxleben in 1777 from a specimen collected at the mouth of the Severn River, Hudson Bay, Ontario, Canada. The genus name means "treasurer squirrel" and is a derivative of the Greek words for "treasurer," *tamias*, and "squirrel," *skiouros*. *Skiouros* literally means "shadow tail" (*skia* means "shadow," and *oura* means "tail"). The genus name is a nod to this squirrel's habit of hoarding food items in large caches. The specific name *hudsonicus* refers to the place where it was first collected. The common name "chickaree" is onomatopoetic with the call these squirrels make.

Two subspecies of red squirrel are found in Arizona: *T. h. mogollonensis*, which is the more widely distributed subspecies, and *T. h. grahamensis*, which is restricted to the Pinaleño Mountains. *T. h. mogollonensis* is named for the Mogollon Rim (Colorado Plateau), and the subspecies *grahamensis* for Mount Graham. They are nearly identical in appearance. Red squirrels were first documented in Arizona by Edgar Mearns, who collected specimens on the Colorado Plateau of central Arizona in 1890 (*T. h. mogollonensis*). The Mount Graham red squirrel, *T. h. grahamensis*, was described by Joel Asaph Allen of the American Museum of Natural History in 1894. Mount Graham red squirrels are federally protected and not open to hunting.

Description: The red squirrel is the smallest of Arizona's tree squirrels, averaging about eight ounces in weight and 13 inches in total length. A very large specimen may weigh as much as a pound and reach more than 14 inches. The ears are small and rounded, and the muzzle is abbreviated, giving the squirrel a pug-nosed appearance. The tail is shorter than the length of the body. This squirrel is gray to brownish dorsally and white to light gray ventrally. A white ring surrounds each eye, and there typically is some white on the muzzle. A rusty red "stripe" runs down the center of the back. This stripe is diffused, often giving the whole dorsum a rusty or brownish appearance. A band of dark fur separates the darker dorsum from the light underparts. The tail is not as bushy as that of other Arizona tree squirrels. It is colored like the animal's dorsum but usually a little darker, and fringed in white.

Habitat and Range in Arizona: Red squirrels are associated with spruce-fir habitats, typically above 7,500 feet elevation; they reach their greatest abundance in Arizona above 8,000 feet. Red squirrels may follow stringers of spruce-fir habitat down cool, moist canyons to lower elevations. They are found on the Kaibab Plateau and in the Chuska Mountains in the northern extremes of our state. They extend across the  Mogollon Rim from the San Francisco Mountains eastward through the White Mountains to New Mexico. Red squirrels also are found in the higher elevations of the Pinaleño Mountains (Mount Graham), where they are protected. This represents the southernmost extension of their distribution.

These squirrels prefer mature forests where the crowns of trees interlock. Trees most often associated with this species are Engelmann spruce, blue spruce, Douglas-fir, white fir, ponderosa pine, bristlecone pine, limber pine, and white pine.

Biology: Red squirrels feed primarily on the seeds and buds of coniferous trees. They also utilize the male cones of pines, spruces, and firs; fungi; the cambium of conifers; tree sap; insects; baby birds; and carrion. Excess food is stored (buried) in large middens, which may be several feet or more in diameter and are made up of debris from stripped cones. This habit of storing large amounts of food makes red squirrels unique among North American squirrels. Middens are constructed in deep shade or other cool, moist situations, typically at the bases of large trees. These middens act like refrigerators, keeping food stores viable for future use. Middens are defended from the trespasses of other squirrels, and each squirrel has one midden that serves as its primary storage site.

Nests are constructed on branches near the tree trunk, usually on the south side of the tree, and are made of grasses, twigs, lichen, and leaves. Red squirrels also nest in tree cavities. More than one nest may be constructed by an individual squirrel. As with other species, the female becomes receptive for only one day a year and

may be pursued by many eager suitors. Breeding takes place in the spring, probably stimulated by the availability of nutrient-rich tree flowers, as in other Arizona squirrels. Young are born in April through July. Red squirrels are much more fecund than other Arizona squirrels and may produce up to seven young. Some biologists believe red squirrels may produce more than one litter per year. Litter size averages between two and four pups. Young are weaned in about a month and a half, and then set out to establish their own territory.

Red squirrel populations fluctuate in response to environmental conditions, such as abundance of food. They are considered common in areas of prime habitat in Arizona. Densities may be as high as one squirrel per acre when conditions are ideal, but one squirrel per five acres is more commonly encountered.

Red squirrels have been documented living up to 10 years in the wild, though half that span is closer to the norm. Most squirrels die during the first year, and very few live past the second.

Habits: These squirrels are compulsive foragers. They have been documented cutting 29 cones in a one-minute period. A near-constant rain of cones often signifies a foraging red squirrel. Much of a squirrel's activity centers on the midden. When snows deepen, the squirrel digs tunnels beneath the snow to maintain access to this precious food resource. Middens may be passed on from generation to generation, growing all the while.

Red squirrels also are notoriously noisy. They boldly and vigorously scold one another and just about any other intruder in their domain. It is not uncommon for interlopers to find a red squirrel chattering overhead nearly as soon as they enter the spruce-fir belt. Many a turkey hunter has been dogged by these small squirrels while attempting to move silently through the woods.

Red squirrel activity is greatest in the morning and late afternoon during warm months, but extends throughout the day, with a peak at midday in winter. Inclement weather stifles activity. Regardless, under most situations, red squirrels are bold and readily observed, though they frequent thickly forested and dimly lit habitats.

Hunting Tips: The small size of this squirrel makes it a less desirable game species than its larger cousins. Hunter surveys show red squirrels historically represent roughly 10% of the squirrels taken in Arizona. Hunting red squirrels is not much different than hunting other squirrel species. Concentrating efforts in appropriate habitats is important, no matter which species is being pursued. Look for middens and other sign of red squirrels. Listen for scolding and chatter from vocalizing squirrels and watch for movement in the trees. See earlier discussions on pursuing squirrels for techniques.

Gear: Binoculars are less likely to be useful for this species, due to its bold nature. Shotguns are effective for red squirrels. The smaller gauges are more than adequate for these pretty little mammals, so a 20-gauge, 28-gauge, or .410-bore shotgun shooting shot sizes of No. 8 or 9 should perform well. Consider using a scoped .22-caliber rifle. This is the most sporting and fun way to take squirrels of any kind and affords the opportunity to place shots to minimize damage to the meat, an important advantage with this smaller species. A scope proves useful in the low light conditions in which these squirrels are often encountered. Camouflage is not necessary, but drab or dark clothing helps the hunter blend in while sitting in wait. Choose comfortable, durable shoes and clothing appropriate for the weather: It can be quite cool at 9,000 feet in fall.

Other Species: Dusky grouse and Nuttall's cottontail also inhabit the spruce-fir forests where red squirrels are found. Spruce-fir north-facing slopes and canyons bring red squirrels into lower elevations, where they come into contact with Abert's squirrels. For the most part, band-tailed pigeons have abandoned red squirrel habitat by the time the hunting season has started.

Rabbits and Hares, Family Leporidae

A black-tailed jackrabbit is all ears and legs.

Along with the closely related pika, rabbits and hares compose the order Lagomorph. Due to their large incisors, lagomorphs are often confused with rodents, from which they differ in several ways. Perhaps the most notable of these is the presence of four upper incisors (close examination reveals a very small set behind the more prominent foremost set) and differences in the structure of the reproductive organs of males.

"Rabbit" is most often used as a general term and includes several different genera of small mammals belonging to the family Leporidae. This family is represented in both the Old and New World. Five different species of two different genera are found in Arizona: *Lepus* (hares) and *Silvilagus* (rabbits). Hares differ from rabbits in that young are born fully furred, with eyes open, and are able to care for themselves shortly after birth. Additionally, hares do not use burrows when giving birth. Rather, they construct a shallow depression lined with grass or use shelters in thickets of grass or shrubs.

Rabbits, on the other hand, are born hairless, with their eyes closed, and typically in an elaborately constructed nest in a burrow or covered depression. Rabbits have a much longer developmental period than hares do.

Though all species of lagomorph are open to take by the hunter, only cottontails are classified as game animals in Arizona. Three species of cottontail are found in our state. They differ subtly from one another, chiefly in body and ear size. The eastern and desert cottontails overlap in distribution, while Nuttall's cottontail is largely confined to the higher elevations of the east-central and northeastern portions of our state. When addressed from the perspective of elevation, desert cottontails occur at the lowest elevations, while Nuttall's cottontails occur at the highest. Eastern cottontails inhabit elevations in between. Cottontails offer an excellent supplement to the hunter's bag and are succulent table fare.

It should be noted that lagomorphs have been known to carry the bacterial disease tularemia (also known as "rabbit fever"). Exposure to the disease generally takes place as the animal is being cleaned, when the bacteria enter the human body through a cut or abrasion. It is recommended that hunters wear rubber gloves when cleaning rabbits and hares and properly cook the meat, which destroys the bacteria.

Rabbits—Cottontails: Genus *Silvilagus*

Introduction: The genus name *Silvilagus* was coined by John Edward Gray in 1867. It means "forest hare." *Sylva* is Latin for "forest," and *lagos* is Greek for "hare."

Desert Cottontail *(Sylvilagus audubonii)*

Other Names: cottontail, Audubon's cottontail

Name: The desert cottontail was originally described as *Lepus audubonii* in 1858 by biologist Spencer Fullerton Baird from specimens collected during the 1853–56 railroad route surveys. Baird, who worked for the Smithsonian Institution, oversaw many of the biological surveys of the time. As Baird wrote in the original description, the species name was given to honor John James Audubon: "I have therefore given it the name of John James Audubon, the world-renowned naturalist, artist, and author—the honored teacher, friend, and benefactor of the writer of these pages." Three subspecies occur in Arizona: *S. a. arizonae, S. a. minor,* and *S. a. warreni.* The subspecific *arizonae* means "from Arizona." The subspecific *minor* means "small or lesser." The subspecific *warreni* was given in honor of western ornithologist and mammalogist Edward Royal Warren.

Description: A medium-sized cottontail, this animal averages 15 inches in length. The female is slightly larger than the male. A large adult can weigh just over two pounds. The ears of this species are proportionally larger than those of other Arizona cottontails. The nape of the neck is rusty orange or brown. The overall color is grizzled gray to brown above and white below. The tail, when viewed from the top, is dark with little or no rufous color and has a broad white margin.

Habitat and Range in Arizona: Found throughout the state, with the exception of the Kaibab Plateau and Mogollon Rim, this rabbit is seldom encountered in pine forests. It is encountered in pinyon-juniper habitats on occasion. Desert cottontails are most often associated with habitats at elevations below 5,000 feet. They frequent areas of dense vegetation, such as those found along the edges of washes and agricultural fields. They often are associated with mesquite, blue and yellow paloverde, ironwood, hackberry, sagebrush, manzanita, wolfberry, gray thorn (lotebush), flat-top buckwheat, little-leaf bursage, creosote, saguaro, pricklypear, and grasses.

Biology: Desert cottontails breed from January through August, and perhaps as late as September, over much of Arizona. Some biologists believe this species may breed year-round in some of our lowest elevations. A single rabbit may produce as many as five litters a year. Nests are constructed in shallow burrows lined with fur or grass and cuttings from other plants. Two to five young are born blind and hairless after 28 days of gestation. The mother is away from the nest often and plugs it with debris when she is absent. She nurses the young about once a day by squatting or lying over the nest opening. The young develop quickly, leaving the nest in 10 to 14 days. They spend the following few weeks of life nearby. Sexual maturity is reached about two and a half months after birth.

Cottontails feed on a variety of plants, ranging from agricultural crops such as alfalfa to wild plants such as mesquite and paloverde leaves and branch tips, succulent annuals, herbaceous perennials, grasses, and pricklypear cactus.

Habits: Cottontails frequent areas that provide abundant shelter. They often hide in the dense vegetation adjacent to fallow or working agricultural areas and washes. They also shelter in tumbleweed patches, brush piles and woodpiles, and beneath the foundations of buildings (especially abandoned ones), rock piles, thickets, and all conceivable places that could hide an animal their size. Cottontails rest in small hollows known as "forms," which they construct in the surrounding vegetation or beneath objects. Rabbits show a great fidelity to cover sites, and home ranges are relatively small. Males spend their lives in areas about 15 acres in size. Home ranges of females are much smaller.

Desert cottontails are shy and secretive. They often freeze when confronted with an uncertain threat, but they flee to cover at the first real sign of danger. Running cottontails seldom stop until they reach cover. They are predominantly nocturnal, but also are active in early morning and late afternoon. Diurnal activity is greatest at dawn and dusk. Much of their foraging is done under the cover of dense vegetation or after dark. Fleeing rabbits run in a zigzag motion, with the white underside of the tail exposed.

Hunting Tips: Desert cottontails are sporting animals to hunt and lots of fun. They also are one of the tastiest small game animals in the state. Search for cottontails along weed-choked field edges. Walk thick cover, such as tumbleweed patches and dry agricultural pump backs. Quail hunters are likely to encounter cottontails most anytime, but especially along desert washes and thickets. Use binoculars from a

distance to search for rabbits in abandoned farmyards or areas near thickets or other cover sites. Upon locating rabbits, pursue them by walking through or near cover to flush them, or take shots from a distance with a scoped .22 rifle. These small rifles offer an excellent challenge and good practice for upcoming big-game hunts. Walking ridgetops in the early morning and late afternoon, using binoculars to search for rabbits in the washes below, can also be an effective way to search for cottontails.

The use of bow and arrow is particularly effective on cottontails, as they often freeze before running, which gives the archer a chance for a close shot. Move cautiously through cottontail habitat, often pausing to visually search nearby cover for concealed rabbits.

Dress bagged rabbits at the first opportunity and put on ice. Occasionally, rabbits are the host to the large grub of the botfly. These unpleasant-looking grubs may be encountered when rabbits are being dressed or when they exit the carcass of a dead rabbit. They do not harm the meat of the rabbit, and no rabbit should be discarded because of them.

Gear: Cottontails are not particularly tough and can be taken with a variety of weapons, including the bow and arrow, which is popular with many sportspeople. Special blunt tips on arrows work very well, as do more typical points. Sitting rabbits make challenging targets, and running rabbits nearly impossible ones. Even bows with light pull-weights are effective on cottontails. Smaller gauges of shotgun work well for rabbits. Shotguns ranging in size from 20-gauge to .410-bore and shooting No. 7½ to 8 shot are more than adequate. The .22-caliber rifle works particularly well for rabbits, but the shooter must be careful that a shot can be safely taken. You are likely to find thick-faced brush pants welcome when working tumbleweeds, catclaw acacia, or other cover cottontails frequent. A game vest also is of great utility for holding bagged rabbits and ammunition while in the field. A good pair of leather boots ensures that cactus does not become a problem and allows the hunter to focus on rabbits rather than foot placement.

Other Species: This widespread and abundant rabbit shares its habitat with numerous other small game species. Gambel's and scaled quail co-inhabit many of Arizona's desert cottontail haunts. Mourning and white-winged doves often feed and roost in areas where cottontails like to hide. River-bottom habitat or pond edges, where rabbits feed and hide, could potentially provide resting areas for ducks, geese, and snipe.

Eastern Cottontail *(Sylvilagus floridanus)*

Other Names: cottontail, gray rabbit

Name: The eastern cottontail was originally named *Lepus sylvaticus* by naturalist and preacher John Bachman in 1837, but the name had already been given to another animal, so it did not stand. This species was renamed by biologist Joel Asaph Allen in 1890. The specific name *floridanus* is a reference to Florida, where the type specimens were collected. Two subspecies occur in Arizona: *S. f. hesperius* and *S. f. holzneri.* The subspecies name *hesperius* is derived from the Latin word for the evening star, *hesperus*. The subspecies name *holzneri* was given in honor of collector Frank X. Holzner, who accompanied Mearns on the Mexican Boundary Surveys in the late 1890s, collecting mammals.

Description: The eastern cottontail is the largest species of cottontail in the state. A female rabbit is slightly larger than a male. A large eastern cottontail may reach three pounds in weight and 17 inches in length. However, weights just over two pounds are probably closer to average for Arizona. This rabbit is gray to brown above, with white underparts. Its ears are proportionally smaller than the desert cottontail's. The tail, when viewed from the top, is dark with some rufous color, and has a narrow white border.

Habitat and Range in Arizona: Eastern cottontails range from the south rim of the Grand Canyon, across the central part of the state, to the southeastern corner. They are predominantly a species of mid-elevation habitats and often are associated with mountain slopes. They occupy habitats below those used by Nuttall's cottontail and, for the most part, above those used by desert cottontails. Eastern  cottontails frequent mesquite and oak grasslands in the southeastern part of the state and pinyon-juniper and chaparral habitats elsewhere. Vegetative associations include pinyon, juniper, live oaks, mesquite, manzanita, scrub oak, mountain mahogany, sugar sumac, and various grasses.

Biology: The phrase "breed like rabbits" could well have been coined in reference to these prolific animals. Eastern cottontails in Arizona have been found with developing young from February through August, but it is likely this species breeds year-round at these southern latitudes. Litter size in Arizona ranges from two to four (up to six or more in other parts of their distribution) after a gestation of about 28 days. These rabbits have been reported to bear up to seven litters per year. Eastern cottontails in northern parts of their distribution have fewer litters per year, but the litters are larger in size. Biologists estimate female eastern cottontails in some parts of their range can produce more than 30 offspring a year.

Young are born in shallow nests dug into the ground. The nest is lined with fur and grass, and like the desert cottontail, the female eastern cottontail plugs the nest to protect the young when she is away. The kits typically are nursed in the morning and again in the evening. Young leave the nest in 10 to 20 days and can care for themselves five weeks after birth. Adult size is reached in about five months. Cottontails born early in the year breed later the same year, though the litter size of these young mothers is smaller than that of larger females. A female who has just given birth may mate again the same day.

If it were not for the high mortality rate of these rabbits, we would be wading waist-deep in them. Though they are capable of living up to 10 years, the average life span of wild eastern cottontails is about 15 months.

Habits: Like other cottontails, this species is crepuscular in habits. Greatest activity for eastern cottontails occurs in the first few hours after sunrise and from sundown to an hour or so after dark. This species also has been known to move about on moonlit nights. Eastern cottontails typically are associated with brushy mountain slopes in Arizona. They prefer to shelter in brush or rock piles, thickets, and similar situations. Small hollows called "forms," which closely approximate the rabbit's dimensions, are made among thick vegetation. These forms are used for resting, and quickly vacated when the rabbit is disturbed.

Home ranges for this species vary from two to six acres, depending on sex and time of year. Males, as with many mammal species, travel farther than females. Male rabbits move less during non-breeding months. This species does not have a territory it defends against others of its kind. Many rabbits may have overlapping home ranges, and may occur in surprising numbers under optimal habitat conditions. Densities of up to 20 rabbits per three acres have been recorded in some habitats in the eastern United States. These rabbits use well-defined lanes for traveling around a home range. Fleeing animals follow these lanes as they move to adequate escape cover.

Elaborate and convoluted courting, mating, dominance, and social behaviors are well-documented for this species. Such interactions include chases, boxing, jumping, face-offs, grooming, leapfrog displays, and various submission and dominance postures. Dominant males breed with most of the available females. The actual mating act may last from as little as 10 seconds to up to several minutes.

This species feeds on a variety of woody and soft-stemmed plants. In most areas, herbaceous annual and perennial plants are eaten during warm months. At these times, various grasses and succulent species such as dandelion and wild alfalfa are favored foods. During winter months, woody plant species compose the bulk of the diet.

Hunting Tips: Search for these rabbits in chaparral or on wooded mountain slopes. Work brushy areas with the idea of pushing hiding rabbits from cover to a spot where a shot can be taken. Flushed rabbits are best taken with a shotgun. Eastern cottontails may be seen in early morning or late afternoon in clearings or openings in brush adjacent to hiding cover. Using binoculars to search for foraging rabbits and stalking in close enough for a shot with a .22 rifle is good practice for big-game hunts.

Clean and cool down bagged rabbits as soon as possible to prevent spoilage. Rabbits often serve as hosts to a large grub, the larvae of the botfly. Grubs may be encountered when rabbits are being dressed. Botfly larvae do not harm the meat of the rabbit and no rabbit should be discarded because of them.

Gear: Cottontails can be taken with a variety of weapons. Use of the bow and arrow is a popular and sporting way to hunt rabbits of all sorts. Even those with the lightest pull-weights work fine. Shotguns of all gauges are suitable when pursuing rabbits. The lighter gauges such as .410-bore to 20-gauge shotguns shooting No. 7½ to 8 shot are excellent choices. A scoped .22-caliber rifle is an effective rabbit-harvesting tool. Though running rabbits can be nearly impossible to hit with any weapon, .22-caliber rifles are downright deadly on rabbits sitting at 50 yards and more. Be careful to ensure any shot can be taken safely.

Brush pants suitable for pushing through thick cover are handy when hunting chaparral habitats. A game vest to hold bagged rabbits and ammunition while in the field is a welcome addition to rabbit-hunting gear. A good, comfortable pair of leather boots helps when negotiating the hilly and sometimes steep environs these rabbits frequent.

Other Species: Oak woodland habitats used by this species are also home to Montezuma quail and mourning doves. High desert grasslands where eastern cottontails are abundant are also frequented by scaled quail, Gambel's quail, and sandhill crane. Ducks and geese rest and feed on stock tanks and in river-bottom habitats where eastern cottontails hide.

Nuttall's Cottontail *(Sylvilagus nuttallii)*

Other Names: mountain cottontail, cottontail

Name: Naturalist and South Carolina Lutheran minister John Bachman described this rabbit in 1837. The specific name *nuttallii* was given in honor of English botanist and zoologist Thomas Nuttall, who worked in the United States until 1841. Two subspecies of Nuttall's cottontail occur in Arizona: *S. n. pinetis*, and *S. n. grangeri*. The subspecies name *pinetis* is derived from the Latin word for pine, *pinus*. The type locality for this subspecies is "White Mountains south of Mount Ord." The subspecies *granger* was named in honor of Walter W. Granger, who later became a paleontologist at the American Museum of Natural History. He collected the first specimen of this subspecies on a paleontological expedition to the Black Hills of South Dakota in 1894.

Description: This species strongly resembles the eastern cottontail. It is a smaller cottontail, with short, rounded ears that have well-furred inner surfaces. The tail is dark above, with a broad rufous band. The hind feet are densely furred. The ventral surfaces, as with other cottontails, are white. The dorsum is brown to gray, often flecked with black or gray, giving it a grizzled appearance. At 14½ inches in length, the female is about an inch longer than the male. A large adult of this species may weigh in excess of a pound and a half.

Habitat and Range in Arizona: The Nuttall's cottontail has a disjunct distribution in our state. It inhabits the north rim of the Grand Canyon and sagebrush and pine habitats in the extreme northeastern corner of the state. It also is found in the White Mountains of east-central Arizona. This rabbit is confined to Arizona's higher elevations. In the White  Mountains, most specimens are encountered in grassy clearings or near rock outcrops in spruce-fir forests at elevations of 7,000 feet and higher. They also are associated with meadows adjacent to aspen stands. In northern Arizona, they frequent elevations lower than those found in the White Mountains and range into sagebrush and ponderosa pine habitats.

Biology: These secretive cottontails are difficult to find and observe. Little is known of their habits in Arizona, and they are poorly studied in many other states where they occur. In Arizona, these rabbits are thought to breed from March though late July and to produce two litters a year. In other areas, they may produce as many as five or more litters a year. A single rabbit may produce 17 or more young a season in these areas. Annual reproduction for Arizona specimens is probably around eight to 12 offspring. Shallow, subterranean nesting burrows often are dug in association with some sort of cover, such as a shrub or downed log. The nest is lined with grass and fur, and covered above with grass, sticks, and other debris by the mother when she leaves. Litter sizes in Arizona range from four to six young. Juvenile females have been documented breeding as early as three months after their birth.

These rabbits feed on sagebrush during winter months in many parts of their range. Grass is the primary summer food resource. Presumably, other forbs also are utilized and are important dietary items.

Habits: Nuttall's cottontails are chiefly crepuscular. They often are found alone. These rabbits spend midday in shelters such as burrows or dense vegetation. Other shelter sites include fallen logs, debris piles, and rock outcrops. This species seems to be less easily alarmed than other cottontails. When disturbed, they have been observed to flee 15 yards or less before stopping, usually behind a shrub or other cover. If pursued, this rabbit has been noted to flee in an arc, rather than a direct line from its pursuer.

Foraging typically takes place under the shelter of dense vegetation or in woodland clearings close to cover.

Hunting Tips: Hunt for this rabbit in or adjacent to spruce-fir-aspen habitats in the places where they occur. Search cover in the vicinity of rock piles and outcrops for hiding rabbits. Walk the edges of meadows, keeping an eye out for downed logs or other debris that may shelter rabbits. Glassing high-elevation meadow edges or forest openings in early morning and late afternoon for foraging rabbits is a good strategy.

Field dress bagged rabbits at the earliest opportunity and cool them down. Occasionally, rabbits are the host to the large grub of the botfly. Though unpleasant-looking, these grubs are harmless and do not affect the edibility of

the rabbit. These grubs are usually encountered when the rabbit is being cleaned or occasionally when they exit the carcass of a bagged rabbit. No rabbit should be discarded because of them.

Gear: Binoculars are helpful for spotting rabbits at a distance along the edges of meadows and clearings. Light boots should be sufficient for negotiating most Nuttall's cottontail habitats. Depending on the time of year, a coat may be a welcome addition to hunting gear. A game vest for holding bagged game and ammunition also comes in handy. Just about any smaller-sized firearm is suitable for hunting rabbits, but a .22-caliber rifle or pistol can make hunting rabbits even more fun and challenging, and is very effective on these small animals. Shotguns from .410-bore to 20-gauge are perfect for rabbits. Shells loaded with shot sizes from No. 8 to 7½ work fine. Many people enjoy hunting rabbits with bow and arrow; certainly this is one of the oldest methods for taking cottontails. Blunt-tipped arrows work very well on rabbits, as do other hunting tips. This rabbit's habit of stopping within 15 yards makes it particularly well-suited for archery hunters.

Other Species: Much of Nuttall's cottontail habitat is also red squirrel and dusky grouse habitat. Occasionally, band-tailed pigeons can be found at higher elevations when the season opens, but this is atypical.

Hares—Jackrabbits: Genus *Lepus*

Introduction: Both species of Arizona jackrabbits belong to the genus *Lepus*, which is Latin for "hare." Jackrabbits are much larger than cottontails and are lanky in build, with very long ears. Though jackrabbits are not designated game animals, they are a popular point of focus for many hunters, and as such, they warrant discussion in this book. They are open to hunting year-round, and there is no bag or possession limit. Despite the absence of bag limits on these animals, it is incumbent on us as hunters to take only what we will use. The flesh of jackrabbits is darker than that of cottontails and makes excellent meatballs or stews.

Black-tailed Jackrabbit *(Lepus californicus)*

Other Names: jackrabbit, jack, desert jackrabbit, blacktail jack

Name: Zoologist John Edward Gray described the black-tailed jackrabbit in 1835. The specific name *californicus* means "from California." The common name refers to this animal's black tail-top. Three subspecies of black-tailed jackrabbit are reported to occur in Arizona: *L. c. texianus*, *L. c. eremicus*, and *L. c. deserticola*. The subspecies name *texianus* means "from Texas." *Eremicus* is derived from the Greek *eremia*, which means "solitude, desert, or wilderness." The subspecific *deserticola* has Latin roots and means "desert-dweller."

Description: This large, short-furred rabbit has long legs and long, oversized ears with black tips. The coat color is grizzled gray to brown dorsally, grading into brown or gray on the sides. The hind feet are large, and the small tail is black on top and white below. The amber-colored eyes are large, and situated high on the head. The undersides are white. An adult specimen may weigh nearly six pounds and stretch two feet in length from nose to tail. The female averages a little larger than the male.

Habitat and Range in Arizona: Black-tailed jackrabbits are statewide in distribution. They are found from desertscrub to conifer woodlands. These rabbits reach their greatest abundance in open desert or semidesert habitats that consist of low shrubs, cacti, and infrequent trees. Plants they are commonly associated with include junipers, mesquite, paloverde, saguaro, buckhorn cholla, bursage, sagebrush, and various grasses.

Biology: Black-tailed jackrabbits first appeared as a species in the late Pliocene or early Pleistocene. They are the most commonly represented fossil hare in North America. And indeed, they are still common and widespread today. These hares produce two types of fecal pellets. One is harder and drier than the other. Discarded as waste, these are the dark, round, slightly flattened pellets generally encountered in the field. The second type of fecal pellet is green, moister, softer, and produced when jacks are resting. These pellets also have more than three times greater protein content than the first kind of pellet, and are ingested by the animal. Discarded pellets may persist in the environment for more than four years. The diet of black-tailed jacks consists of mesquite bark and leaves, cacti, succulent forbs, and the stems and leaves of woody shrubs. Young mesquite leaves are especially favored. Agricultural crops such as wheat and alfalfa are also utilized.

Black-tailed jackrabbits use free water if it's available, but free water is not a necessity and they do not move to and from water sources on a regular basis. Rather, they gain all their needed moisture from food. Much of their diet consists of moist plant matter, and the proportions of these items in their diet increases during dry, hot periods. It has been noted that during such times, the amount of cacti taken increases. Water loss and the effects of extreme temperatures are minimized through not only physiological adaptations, but also behaviors such as seeking shade. These hares can tolerate body temperatures of more than 113 degrees before dying. Shallow forms are constructed in the shade, in which they spend inactive hours and keep as cool as possible. Temperatures in forms measured in Utah averaged a couple of degrees cooler than those outside.

Courtship includes mating chases, jumping, and circling. These animals do not form protracted pair bonds; rather, the female accepts the first male that shows interest. Breeding in Arizona occurs in all months except November. After a 40-day gestation period, two to seven young are born. The female may breed again the same day she gives birth. Nests are shallowly constructed affairs, sometimes lined with fur or plant material. The average litter size in Arizona is two, but this varies depending on the amount of rainfall. Three to six litters per year are birthed by black-tailed jackrabbits in Arizona, with a potential of about 14 young being produced annually. Size and weight of young varies within the litter. One individual is usually substantially larger than the rest. At one day of age, weighing an average of just over two ounces, the young are about 3% of the size of adults. Young are born with teeth, eyes open, and fully furred, and they already sport the black tail-top and ear tips characteristic of adults. The young are nourished exclusively by nursing for the first 10 days of life. After that, nursing is supplemented with solid foods. The mother typically nurses the young at night and moves away from them during the day. Though she remains near her young, should a predator approach, she does not attempt to distract or lead it away. By three days of age, young jacks already exhibit good coordination and have begun to stray from the nest site. However, the mother and litter typically stay close to the birthing site for about a week. The mother hare gathers her young together if they become dispersed.

At eight months, the young have reached adult size and are essentially indistinguishable from their parents. Some research indicates only 9% of the young live beyond the first year, and only 2% survive past their third year. Maximum life expectancy for wild-living jackrabbits is estimated to be around seven years. Populations of these hares are cyclic within a 10-year time frame. Numbers may also increase when predator-control efforts reduce coyote numbers. One study showed coyotes accounted for 64% of the deaths in black-tailed jackrabbits.

SMALL GAME MAMMALS

Habits: Blacktail jacks prefer open areas with scattered low shrubs and cacti. For the most part, they avoid dense grass and shrub communities, where visibility is limited. They can become very abundant in severely overgrazed habitats. These hares are primarily nocturnal but may be active on cloudy days. Home ranges documented for this species ranged from 49 to 345 acres. Black-tailed jackrabbits frequent agricultural areas, where they may reach numbers so great they become pests.

Hearing appears to be one of their most important senses for detecting danger, which is understandable when you consider the size of their ears. When danger is sensed, these hares remain motionless, sneak away, or run. When fleeing, they may attain speeds nearing 40 miles per hour, and often travel in a "U" or "L" pattern, stopping to face potential danger at a right angle. When unsure of the source of danger, these animals may take slow, high bounds while fleeing, in an attempt to sight the potential predator.

These jackrabbits are not social animals but may congregate in large numbers when favored food resources are available. At these times, congregations of 250 individuals have been noted. Black-tailed jackrabbits also may gather in small groups of up to five animals when breeding. Greatest diurnal activity occurs just before dark and in the first few hours of daylight. Individuals can be found resting at midday in the sparse shade of desert shrubs and trees, especially during hot weather.

Hunting Tips: When hunting black-tailed jackrabbits, be quiet. Their keen sense of hearing is their primary defense against potential predators. These hares can be found during the day by scanning appropriate habitat with binoculars, paying particular attention to shaded resting sites such as beneath desert shrubs and trees. Once a black-tailed jackrabbit is located, move toward it in an attempt to approach within gun range. Watch for these hares moving near or along the edges of agricultural fields and the open terrain adjacent to washes, early in the morning and in the last hour of daylight. Walking through appropriate habitats will flush jackrabbits, often at great distances. At these times, they will be seen bounding far ahead. Walking two or three people abreast, spaced 40–60 yards apart moving through good habitat, will push rabbits from cover and likely result in some shots being offered. Walk down old desert roads and trails, searching for resting hares in the distance on either side of the route. Return to the vehicle frequently to clean bagged hares and get them on ice. They make much better table fare if they are well cared for.

Gear: A straight-shooting, scoped .22-caliber rifle is perfect for hunting these large hares. Many shots are taken at greater than 40 yards, and the scope not only proves useful, but at times is essential. A bipod, or some other portable rest, can be handy for holding the rifle steady when attempting one of those epic long shots. Shotguns are certainly useable for jackrabbits, but these firearms are most effective at relatively short ranges. When hunting in areas where shots are likely to occur within 30 yards or less, a shotgun is the ideal choice. Use standard loads of No. 8 to 6 shot to bring down hares. A game vest is handy in transporting bagged jacks, but they are big, and a single animal adds a lot of weight and takes up a lot of space. Walking around with a couple of jacks in a game bag is like hauling around a fair-sized dog. Due to these challenges, make short loops for jackrabbits, returning frequently to your vehicle to deposit game. Brush pants or other stout leg wear, a wide-brimmed hat for sun protection, and a good pair of boots round out the gear list for the jackrabbit hunter.

Other Species: Desert cottontail, mourning and white-winged doves, and Gambel's and scaled quail share the black-tailed jackrabbit's habitat. At the very highest portions of their range, blacktail jacks may occur with Abert's squirrels, though this is rather uncommon.

Antelope Jackrabbit *(Lepus alleni)*

Other Names: antelope jack, jackrabbit, jack, *liebre appaloosa*

Name: Edgar Mearns described this hare in 1890 from specimens collected at Rillito Station north of Tucson. The specific name was given in honor of zoologist Joel Asaph Allen. Interestingly, Allen authored "Allen's Rule" in 1877, and hares in particular are excellent illustrations of his rule. Allen's Rule states that the extremities of mammals (ears, limbs, etc.) from colder climates are smaller (shorter) than those of closely related animals from warmer areas. The antelope jackrabbit is one of the animals that best illustrates this concept. The common name of the antelope jackrabbit is most likely a reference to this species' habit of erecting the white fur on its rump, as a pronghorn does when startled.

Description: The antelope jackrabbit is the largest hare in Arizona. A large individual may attain a length just over 26 inches. Of 60 specimens weighed in February 2011 from southern Arizona, all weighed between 4 ½ and 10 pounds. A female in the advanced stages of pregnancy may approach 13 pounds.

The antelope jackrabbit has long, slender limbs with the large, oversized hind feet typical of jackrabbits. Its conspicuous, beige-tipped ears are a key identification character. The ears are approximately one-third the length of the hare. The dorsum is grizzled gray-brown and the flanks are light gray, becoming lighter toward the rump. When this jackrabbit is startled, the hairs on the flanks are raised, making them appear white. The chest is cinnamon-ochre and the undersides off-white. *Lepus alleni* also sports a very short, light-colored tail one to two inches long. It frequently occurs in small groups. One subspecies of this hare occurs in Arizona: *L. a. alleni.*

Habitat and Range in Arizona: Antelope jackrabbits typically are found below 3,800 feet elevation. Their distribution in the state ranges from the vicinity of Apache Junction and the base of the Superstition Mountains south to the international border, east to the San Pedro River Valley, and west to the vicinity of Organ Pipe Cactus National Monument. There are a couple of records from near Fort Bowie in Cochise County, 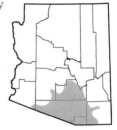 but these hares have not been seen there in years. Antelope jackrabbits inhabit open country, from grasslands to desert flats. They are often associated with mesquite, ironwood, blue paloverde, catclaw, cane cholla (walkingstick cactus), Pima pineapple cactus (long-tubercle beehive cactus), and saguaro, as well as a host of perennial and seasonal grasses.

Biology: Antelope jackrabbits are tropical animals, and their most conspicuous anatomical feature, other than their large size, is their expansive ears. These may represent more than a quarter of the hare's body surface area. These appendages assist in conducting and radiating heat. Coupled with the highly reflective nature of the fur and behaviors that seek to minimize exposure to temperature extremes, the ears help the antelope jackrabbit conserve water by effectively regulating its body temperature. During hot periods, blood flow to the ears is minimized, allowing the jackrabbit to conduct little heat from its surroundings. When temperatures drop below the hare's body temperature, hot blood is channeled through the ears and cooled. When exposed to temperatures of nearly 124 degrees Fahrenheit for several hours, these animals were still able to maintain a stable body temperature.

Until recently, antelope jackrabbits were not known to drink free water. C. T. Vorhies and Walter Taylor, in their extensive research on *Lepus*, never observed them drinking. However, recent trail-camera data indicate this species does drink water, at least occasionally. Most observations have been at night and in late afternoon. The absence of free water does not limit the distribution of this species. Antelope jackrabbits can acquire all the moisture they need by consuming succulent plants, such as cacti, and mesquite leaves. Their consumption of cacti increases as conditions become dryer.

These hares reach sexual maturity during the second year of life. They can produce up to four litters of one to five young between April and October. A shallow, fur-lined nest is constructed beneath sheltering vegetation or some other object. Young are born after a six-week gestation period. In Arizona, the average litter size is about two. The young are born fully furred and with their eyes open, and sport a white spot on the forehead. This spot is lost as the hare matures. The mother suckles the young at night but otherwise stays away from the nest. The young develop quickly and are independent soon after birth.

A study done in 1933 examined the contents of 179 antelope jackrabbit stomachs. It found that nearly half of their diet consisted of grasses (45%), followed by mesquites (36%), cacti (7.8%), and various other vegetation (11.2%). The percentage of these dietary items varies according to rainfall and the resulting availability of forage items. During the rainy season, grasses become more widely available and make up more of the diet. These jackrabbits do not frequent agricultural fields under normal circumstances.

Habits: Antelope jackrabbits may have home ranges of more than 1,500 acres. Densities of up to one hare per five acres can be attained in favorable habitats. On occasion, antelope jackrabbits congregate in large numbers of 20 or more. Though the reason for these gatherings is open to speculation at this point, it may have to do with reproduction or favorable feeding areas. Encountering pairs or small groups of three to eight jacks is not unusual. Antelope jackrabbits can be more common in certain habitats than their more widespread cousins, black-tailed jackrabbits.

Antelope jackrabbits do not construct burrows but make shallow scrapes called "forms" to rest in. They are inactive during excessively hot or otherwise unsuitable conditions. Jacks frequently can be found resting in the shade of a tree, shrub, or cactus. Such localities not only offer some relief from the elements but afford the hare a good vantage point from which to watch for danger, while obscuring it from the view of potential predators. Like other lagomorphs, antelope jackrabbits are most active in the mornings, evenings, and after dark. They venture out from resting cover to feed near dark. Feeding may continue into the midmorning hours or longer during cloudy weather.

Antelope jackrabbits can attain speeds of nearly 45 miles per hour and may well be the fastest of the jackrabbits. When disturbed, they erect the white hair on their flanks and rump and run away from the potential predator. While running, they often make high leaps to pinpoint the source of danger.

Hunting Tips. Antelope jackrabbits, like other jackrabbits, have excellent hearing, and it is important to keep unnecessary noise to a minimum when pursuing them. Jackrabbits can be found loafing during the day by using binoculars to scan beneath distant shrubs, cacti, and desert trees. Pay particular attention to shaded resting sites. Once a jackrabbit is located, plan a stalk that will keep you out of view of the

SMALL GAME MAMMALS

hare until firearm range is reached. Then, quietly move toward the target.

Watch for hares moving in the open country adjacent to wash edges early in the morning and in the last hour of daylight. Slowly walking through jackrabbit habitat will flush hares, sometimes far in front of you. These animals may be seen bounding off in the distance. Sometimes, a fleeing jackrabbit can be made to stop by loudly whistling at it. An often-successful strategy for hunting jackrabbits is for two or three people to walk abreast, spaced about 40 to 60 yards apart. Move slowly and quietly through good habitat to push jacks from cover. Flushing hares in this manner often results in one or more party members getting a shot. Also, try hiking quietly down old two-tracks and trails, searching for resting hares in the distance. When game is bagged during warm weather, return to the vehicle and clean the game. Put it on ice as soon as possible. It makes much better table fare if well cared for.

Gear: Probably the most effective and fun weapon to use for jackrabbits is a .22-caliber rifle. A low-power scope is a nearly must-have item, as shots often exceed 40 yards. Having a good, steady rest increases accuracy and is essential for consistently making long shots. A bipod, monopod, or some other portable rest provides a solid base to shoot from. Due to the longer shooting distances usually encountered when hunting jackrabbits, you will find a shotgun a less effective weapon than a rifle, but if you hunt an area where shots at hares are likely to occur within 30 yards or less, a shotgun is a good choice. Use standard loads of No. 8 to 6 shot: Even big antelope jackrabbits are not especially tough. A game vest will help you carry these large hares back to your vehicle. You may consider a sling or game carrier to transport bagged antelope jackrabbits. Due to these challenges, make short forays in the field for jacks, returning to your vehicle to deposit game as you bag it. Brush pants, a wide-brimmed hat, and a good pair of boots complete the essentials for hunting jacks.

Other Species: These large hares may occur with Gambel's and scaled quail. Mourning doves roost and loaf in thickets in antelope jackrabbit habitat. Black-tailed jackrabbits can sometimes be found in the same habitat.

From Field to Table

Introduction to Caring for and Cooking Small Game

What to do after you bring the animal to hand can be a mysterious, confusing, and frustrating question. There are multiple methods for cleaning and cooking each type of game animal, and though these are mostly common sense, a few tips and shortcuts can help make this job quick and easy. In this section, I describe the methods I most often employ, but I encourage you to experiment and talk with other hunters to find the approach that best suits your needs.

One of the most important aspects of transforming bagged game into a savory meal is proper field care. Any harvested wildlife can quickly become unpalatable if mistreated. Think of wildlife you've taken as you would a fresh steak purchased from your local grocer, and care for it in much the same way.

Tools for processing small game are fairly basic. A sharp pocketknife is all you need in most instances. Game shears are a handy and useful tool for removing legs, wings, and heads. Place processed game in plastic bags suitable for refrigeration or freezing, or set it in a bowl of water in the refrigerator if it is to be prepared within a day or two. Rubber gloves of the type found in most hardware stores are a handy item and minimize cleanup after the job is done.

No matter what the size or type of game, it is important to cool it as quickly as reasonably possible. For the very best results on the table, it should be field dressed (skinned, eviscerated, and washed), then cooled after it is killed. Keeping an ice chest on hand will greatly facilitate this process.

Care and Cleaning of Birds

"Cleaning" is the term generally given to preparing fish or game for cooking. It entails removing all inedible parts prior to preparing meat for the table. There are three general approaches to processing birds: plucking, skinning, or filleting the meat off the breast. The majority of birds can be processed almost if not entirely without tools.

Regardless of which approach you take, you will need to remove some of the bird's extremities before, during, or after processing. Often, you will find it easier to leave the head, wings, or legs on the bird until after it has been processed. I give the various steps in the order I find most helpful. You may prefer to rearrange the order to suit you. The procedure is basically the same for all similarly sized birds, regardless of the species.

Removing the wings: Wings can be removed by three methods: by clipping the wings off near their junction with the body with a pair of shears, by breaking them off near their junction with the body, or by separating the wing at the elbow joint and cutting it off. The wings of large birds such as ducks can be very difficult to break by hand. But on small birds such as doves and quail, I generally break the wings off. To break the wing of a small bird, take the bird's humerus (the bone closest to the bird's body) in both hands, grasping the bone between the second segment of the index finger and the thumb and placing both thumbs tip to tip, as you would if you were snapping a twig or pencil. Push downward with your thumbs while rotating your hands outward, pulling the wing away from the bird's body.

Removing the feet: These generally have to be clipped off with shears or broken in a manner similar to the wings and removed with a knife. You can also twist the leg at the ankle—the first joint on the leg above the toes—separating the joint. Then cut through the tendons with a knife. This has the advantage of not leaving sharp, broken bones protruding from the bird carcass. In all species for which the legs are saved, remove just the scaly part of the leg.

Removing the head: The head is probably the most easily removed bird extremity. On very large birds such as cranes or geese, remove the head with shears or cut off the neck at the juncture with the torso. However, the head of most birds, even fairly large ones, can generally be pulled off by hand. To remove the head, hold the body firmly in one hand and grasp the head in your other fist. Pinch your index finger and thumb together around the bird's neck at the base of the head and pull away from the bird's body with a steady pressure. The head should come off easily.

After the bird is cleaned, wash it with care, paying particular attention to removing embedded feathers and shot pellets.

Plucking

Any bird can be plucked, but I have never particularly enjoyed the task, as it is generally messy and time-consuming. However, a plucked bird often makes excellent table fare and a particularly attractive presentation. Leaving the skin on the bird helps seal in moisture when cooking and adds more flavor. There are those who differ, but I generally don't pluck birds smaller than waterfowl and even then, seldom do this. Admittedly, a plucked and roasted duck stuffed with dressing and wrapped in bacon looks every bit as enticing as it is tasty.

For most birds, plucking is best done with the bird thoroughly wet, to prevent feathers from drifting on the slightest breeze, resulting in a mess. This does not work well with waterfowl, however, and you may want to hold such birds in a trash can while you remove the feathers. To wet a bird, hold it by its feet and dip it in water that is just below the boiling point (step 1). Submerge the bird for about five to 15 seconds, just long enough to get the feathers wet. Then place the wetted bird on a table (step 2). Holding it by the legs, grasp feathers between the index finger and thumb and pull away (step 3). Some find it easiest to start plucking at the neck, while others (including me) start at the opposite end. Pluck the largest feathers first, then the smaller ones. Continue until the bird is free of feathers. Pin and smaller feathers can be either picked off individually, rinsed off (step 4), or singed off by use of a handheld gas torch or a torch made from a tightly rolled cone of newspaper. The head, feet, and wings can now be removed. Disembowel the bird and wash it.

STEP 1

STEP 2

STEP 3

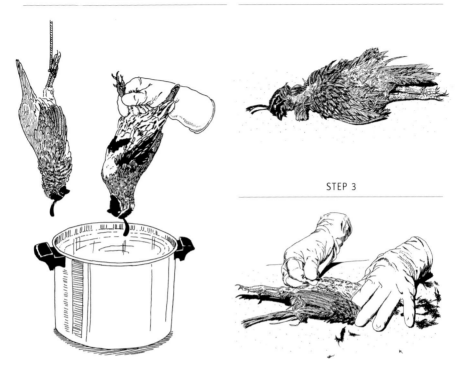

STEP 4

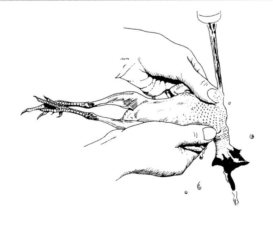

FROM FIELD TO TABLE

Skinning

Rather than plucking birds, I generally skin them. It is a quick, clean, and efficient approach to game care. The process is generally the same for most birds, with some small deviations in the execution. Most small birds are thin-skinned, and the skin easily tears. With larger species, a knife will help in cutting the skin to start the process. After you make the initial incision, the rest of the skin can usually be removed by hand. Start the incision on the breast, not the body cavity. This will make the skinning process easier and less messy. In a nutshell, the step-by-step process for any bird is:

- Remove head.
- Remove wings.
- Remove skin.
- Remove entrails.
- Remove feet.
- Wash bird.

The order of the removal of extremities is largely a matter of personal preference. I like leaving the feet and legs attached until the end, because they make a convenient handle for manipulating the bird.

Skinning quail, grouse, chukars, and pheasants: These are the Arizona game birds that have enough meat on the legs to save for a meal. They are all cleaned in the same way. Remove the head by grasping the body in one hand and the head in the other and pull in a firm steady fashion in opposite directions (step 1). The wings of larger birds are difficult to break and probably require the use of shears or some similar tool. Remove the wings first, but leave the legs in place (step 2). Then hold the bird in one hand and, with the other, pinch the skin on the breast at the base of the neck and pull until it tears (step 3). Pull the torn skin downward, working around the body and peeling the bird until the skin is pulled down around the ankles (where the scales on the legs begin) (step 4). This should be easily accomplished with little mess, as the feathers of these birds are firmly attached. Cut the legs off above the ankles, discarding the feet and skin. Open the body cavity by grasping the keel point of the breast (located between the legs on the belly) with your thumb while holding the carcass in the other hand. Pull upward, opening the body cavity (step 5). Clean out the entrails. Cut off the legs with a knife or shears and wash the bird (step 6).

START

STEP 1

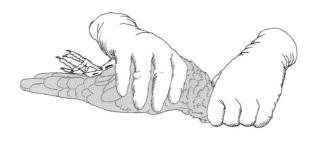

STEP 2

STEP 3

STEP 4

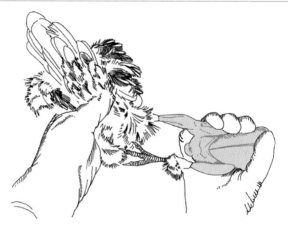

STEP 5

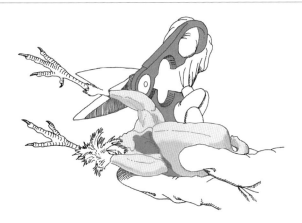

Breasting doves, pigeons, and snipe: These birds have small legs that typically are not worth the effort to save. They are all cleaned the same way. Remove the wings (step 1) and tear the skin near the top of the breast as described previously, exposing the entire breast (step 2). While holding the bird in your opposite hand, grasp the bird at the point of the "V" at the bottom of the breast with your thumb and pull up, opening the body cavity. Slide your thumb into the cavity to the base of the neck. Holding the breast tightly, lift it out of the bird (step 3). The head and the rest of the bird will remain in your other hand. Discard the remains and wash the breast (step 4).

STEP 1	STEP 2

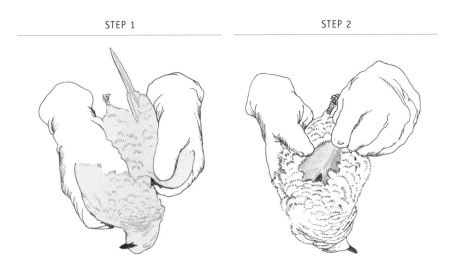

FROM FIELD TO TABLE

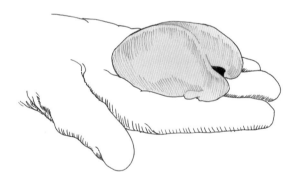

Filleting

This is the approach I most often use for ducks, geese, and cranes. There is little meat on the legs of ducks and geese, so I do not save them. It should be noted that many go through this extra effort, as it could be argued that it is wasteful not to. That is a choice for you to make. However, on cranes, the thighs are quite meaty and you will want to save them. You will need a sharp knife that is easy to manipulate.

Lay the bird on its back. Cut an incision along the center keel of the breast from the "V" at the bottom of the breast to the base of the neck (step 1). Peel the skin back, exposing the entire breast (including the sides to the point where the wings connect) (step 2). Using your knife, cut alongside the keel bone of the breast and follow the horizontal surface of the breast bone (step 3). Grasping the fillet with your other hand as you cut will help in removing the meat (step 4). Cut down the sides of the bird, following the contour of the bone toward the back of the bird as much as possible. When you reach the sides of the bird, where the wings attach to the body and the breastbone ends and the ribs begin, cut the fillet free. With cranes, skin the leg back from the knee until the thigh is exposed from the knee to the upper pelvis of the bird. Cut the lower leg off at the knee by twisting the knee joint until the two bones separate, then use a knife to cut the tendons. Firmly grab the lower portion of the thigh just above the knee joint and rotate the thigh upward until the hip joint separates. Use the knife to fillet the meat from the bird's hip and to separate the hip joint to remove the leg.

STEP 1

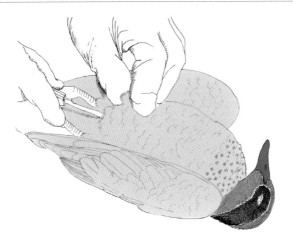

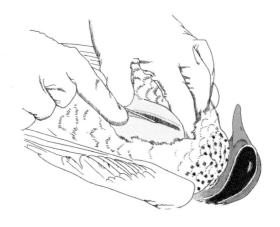

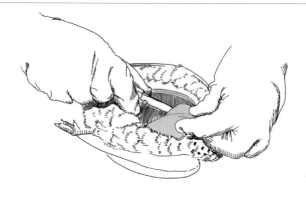

Care and Cleaning of Small Mammals

The basic method for processing all small mammals is the same: skin, then cut into smaller portions if required for table presentation. When removing the hide, try to keep hair off the meat, as it can be difficult to wash off. When dressing small mammals, you will find that some, such as squirrels, have incredibly tough hide, while the skin of others, such as rabbits and hares, can easily be torn by hand. My general approach is to remove the head, tail, and feet after the animal is skinned, as I find these parts useful gripping points for some species. You will need a sharp knife or game shears to process all small game mammals.

Squirrels

Try to skin bagged squirrels as soon as possible after they have been killed. The hide is very tough, and the longer the animal has been dead, the more tenaciously the skin holds to the body. Place the squirrel on its belly and, with a sharp knife, cut the skin at a right angle to the spine at the midpoint of the back (as if you were going to cut the squirrel in half) (step 1). Holding the squirrel crossways in front of you, insert the fingers of both hands beneath the skin on opposite sides of the cut with the knuckles of your hands nearly touching (step 2). Grip tightly and pull until the skin tears and peels back to the squirrel's head, feet, and tail (step 3). Remove the head, tail, and feet (step 4), then open the body cavity by inserting a knife just under the stomach muscle starting between the legs, and cutting upward to the base of the neck (step 5). Try not to puncture any internal organs. After removing the entrails, wash the squirrel thoroughly. This skinning method works particularly well when you have a partner to help. In this instance, each person would grab a portion of skin and the two of you would pull away from each other in a tug-of-war fashion.

STEP 1

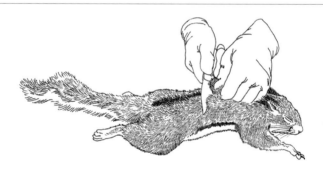

STEP 2

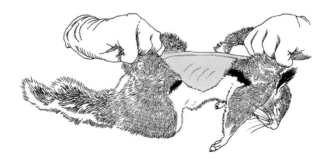

STEP 3

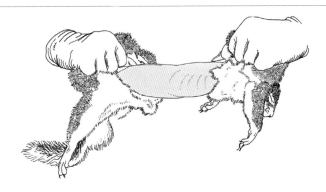

STEP 4

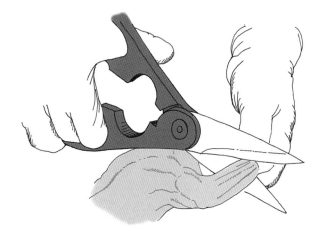

STEP 5

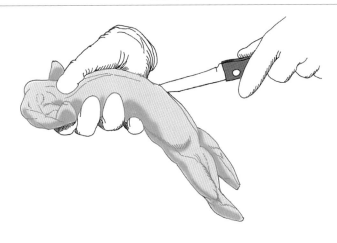

Rabbits and Hares

Hold the rabbit or hare by the ears in one hand (step 1) and, with the other, either cut or tear the skin at the base of the neck (step 2). Rabbit skin is very thin and can easily be torn by pinching it between your fingernails or cutting it with a small knife. Peel the skin downward (step 3) to the ankles of each foot and then pull it off (step 4). The skin will tear off just above the rabbit's foot. Cut off the feet (step 5). Remove the head with a knife or by gripping it tightly in one hand while holding the body firmly in the other. The head can be twisted and torn off with little effort (step 6). Then open the body cavity: Starting just above or between the rear legs, cut upward through the chest cavity to the base of the neck. Try not to puncture any internal organs (step 7). Remove the entrails and wash thoroughly.

STEP 1	STEP 2

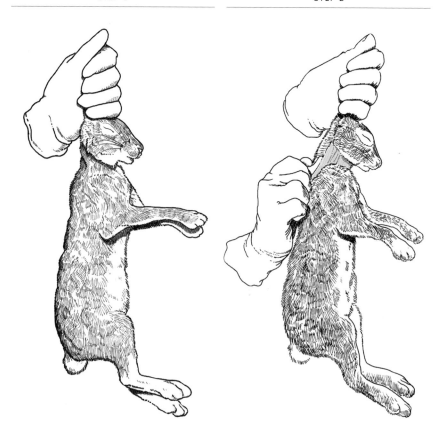

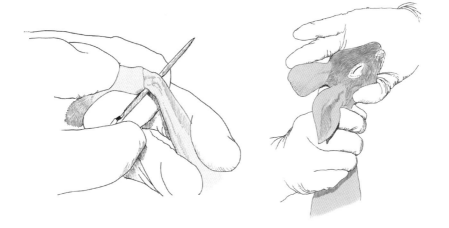

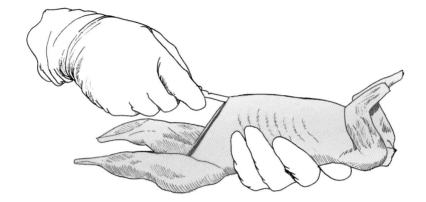

Small Game Recipes

Aside from days in the field, one of the best parts of hunting is enjoying your success with family and friends around the table. The following are a handful of recipes from various sources. Some are old family favorites; others were gleaned from cookbooks or friends. Many of the recipes for white meats such as quail, grouse, rabbit, and squirrel are interchangeable. That is to say, any white game meat can be substituted in those recipes. I hope you enjoy these as much as we have.

Birds

Grilled Marinated Duck

¼ cup Worcestershire sauce
2 tablespoons olive oil
½ teaspoon hot sauce
2 tablespoons minced garlic
¼ teaspoon black pepper
8 skinned, boned duck breast halves

Stir together Worcestershire sauce, olive oil, hot sauce, garlic, and pepper. Add duck breasts, toss well to coat, and cover. Put in the refrigerator for at least 30 minutes to overnight.

Preheat a grill at medium-high heat. Grill the duck to desired doneness, about 5 minutes per side for medium-well depending on the size of the breast and the grill temperature. Note: duck will be more tender if served a little on the rare side.

Duck a l'Orange

1 orange
2 duck breasts
⅓ cup white wine
4 tablespoons orange marmalade
3 tablespoons Dijon mustard
2 beef bouillon cubes
1½ cups heavy cream
Salt
Pepper
Orange zest strips and chopped fresh parsley for garnish

Cut long strips of orange zest using a zester and set aside for garnish. Squeeze the orange and set the juice aside for later use.

Heat a frying pan over high heat and add duck breasts. Sauté, without oil, for about 8 minutes. Turn the breasts and cook for 4 more minutes. Do not overcook: The breasts should be pink inside. Small breasts take less time, so adjust accordingly. Set duck aside and keep warm. Pour off any fat from pan, add wine and deglaze, scraping the browned bits off the bottom. Add the juice from the orange, marmalade, and mustard. Mix well. Add the bouillon cubes and allow to dissolve. Reduce heat and add heavy cream, mixing well; let bubble for a few minutes until thickened. Season to taste with salt and pepper.

Slice duck breasts into ¼-inch slices and arrange in an overlapping fan around the outside of the plate. Pour sauce over the slices and garnish with strips of orange zest and chopped parsley. Serves 2.

Goose Kebabs

2 goose breasts, skinned and filleted of bone and diced in bite-sized pieces

Garlic powder

Seasoned salt

Seasoned pepper

1 cubed onion

1 cubed green pepper

½ pound bacon

1 cubed tomato

Place diced goose in a pan and season to taste with suggested seasonings or your own selection. Refrigerate overnight. Arrange cubed onion, green pepper, tomato, and chunks of goose (wrapped in bacon) on skewer. Heat grill to medium and grill until the goose is brown outside but still pink inside, about 3 minutes or so on each side.

Dove Stew

12 dove breasts, skinned or plucked

Flour

Bacon fat

Vegetables of your choice

2 large potatoes

Cornstarch, mixed with cold water

Dredge doves in flour and fry in bacon fat until brown. Place doves, potatoes, and other vegetables in a large pot, cover, and slow-cook for 4 hours. Add cornstarch, a little at a time, to thicken to desired consistency. (Works well for band-tailed pigeons, too.)

Doves or Band-tails in Foil

12 dove breasts or 6 band-tailed pigeon breasts, skinned or plucked

Seasoned salt

Pepper

Garlic powder

6 to 8 strips of bacon

6 10-inch by 10-inch sheets of aluminum foil

2 potatoes

1 onion

Other vegetables of your choice

Season dove breasts to taste. Cut bacon strips in half and wrap each breast in bacon strips, covering the whole breast (hold bacon in place with toothpicks if necessary). Cut six 10-inch by 10-inch sheets of foil. Place 2 sheets together, making 3 double sheets of foil. Place 4 dove breasts in the center of each double sheet and surround with chunked potatoes and onions (add other vegetables such as green peppers if desired). Season vegetables to taste. Seal doves and vegetables in foil and place on cooking sheet in oven at 325 degrees. Cook for 45 minutes. Serves 3.

No Fail Quail

4 quail

Salt and pepper

2 tablespoons melted butter

2 tablespoons flour

1 can consommé

¼ teaspoon thyme

1½ bay leaves

1 cup dry white wine

Split quail down the back and flatten. Salt and pepper lightly, then brown slowly in melted butter in a skillet. Sprinkle flour over the birds. Add consommé, thyme, bay leaves, and wine. Bring to a bubble, cover, and simmer until tender, about 30 to 40 minutes. Put pan juices into a dish and spoon over the quail. This dish is delicious paired with wild rice. The recipe works well on doves, too.

Quail and Wild Rice

8 quail

Seasoned salt

Pepper

Garlic powder

1 tablespoon oil

2 cups parboiled wild rice

1 package dry onion soup mix

½ cup water

Season quail to taste and brown in hot oil. Parboil wild rice per directions on package until almost done. Place a layer of rice into an 8-inch by 12-inch casserole dish and lay quail on top. Pack the remaining rice around the birds, filling the body cavities. Sprinkle the package of onion soup mix over the top. Pour water over the soup. Cover dish and place in oven for 20 to 30 minutes at 325 degrees.

Fried Grouse

1 to 4 grouse, cut into serving-sized pieces

Flour (optional)

2 tablespoons oil

1 teaspoon pepper

1 teaspoon seasoned salt

1 teaspoon garlic powder

½ cup water, chicken broth, or wine

Place seasonings and flour in a paper or plastic bag with grouse parts and shake. If you don't want to flour the pieces, merely season them to taste. Place seasoned grouse in skillet with hot oil and brown. A large electric skillet works well for this. After bird is browned, add water, broth, or wine to skillet, turn heat to low, cover, and simmer for 45 minutes to an hour or until tender.

Grouse Casserole

2 grouse

5–6 tablespoons of butter

1 minced clove garlic

4 shallots finely diced

¼ teaspoon basil

1 cup button mushrooms

2 cups dry white wine

½ cup flour

1 dash Tabasco sauce

1 tablespoon minced parsley

¼ pound thinly sliced Italian ham (prosciutto)

Salt

Freshly ground black pepper

1 cup sour cream

Disjoint the two grouse and rub the sections with salt and pepper, then lightly dust with flour. In a large skillet, melt butter, and when hot, add the grouse sections along with the diced livers, hearts, and gizzards. Sauté grouse sections until light brown, then remove, leaving hearts, livers, and gizzards in the skillet.

Line the bottom and sides of an earthenware casserole with paper-thin slices of Italian ham. Arrange the grouse sections in the bottom of the casserole. To the hearts, livers, and gizzards, add shallots and garlic clove and sauté for 2 or 3 minutes. Then add 1 cup of dry white wine, button mushrooms, parsley, basil, and a dash of Tabasco sauce. Bring to a boil and pour over the grouse in the casserole. Add the other cup of wine and place cover on the casserole. Cook for 1½ hours in a 350-degree oven. Carefully stir in the sour cream, return to the oven for 5 minutes, then remove and serve.

Pigeon Andros

8 pigeons or doves

3 cups cooked wild rice

1 cup chopped button mushrooms

1 cup dry white wine

1 wineglass of port
(Madeira can be substituted)

½ cup fresh lime juice

5–6 tablespoons butter

½ teaspoon rosemary

2 shallots, minced

Thyme

Salt

Freshly ground pepper

In a small saucepan, melt 2 tablespoons of butter and use it to lightly brown shallots. Add 2 pinches of thyme, salt and pepper, port, and button mushrooms. Bring to boil, remove from heat, and stir in cooked wild rice.

Rub pigeons with salt and freshly ground black pepper, inside and out. Stuff birds with wild rice, then rub thoroughly with butter and place in a shallow roasting pan. In a saucepan, place dry white wine, rosemary, lime juice, and the remainder of the butter. Bring to a boil, then remove from heat.

Place pigeons in an oven preheated to 500 degrees for 5 minutes, reduce the heat to 350 degrees, and cook for 25 minutes, basting very frequently with the wine–lime juice–butter mixture. Baste with the drippings when this is used up.

Remove the pigeons to a warming oven, place the roasting pan over a low flame, and add ½ cup of water, stirring and scraping the pan until the gravy thickens. Pour over the pigeons and serve.

Mammals

Squirrelitos

This recipe was created with taquitos in mind and feeds a good number of people. It turned out to be a unique, plentiful, and tasty food item to serve at a party for carnivores.

I started with an approximately 10-pound block of frozen, cleaned, and skinned squirrel carcasses. Make this recipe your own by using more or less meat, and fresh or frozen squirrels. The most important thing is to simmer them for a long time in a rich broth (chicken is recommended). Don't be afraid of adding more ingredients and seasoning to your taste!

5 pounds of thoroughly cleaned, skinned squirrels

Homemade chicken broth (below)

Olive and canola or corn oil

Corn tortillas (2 dozen or more)

1 to 2 onions, chopped

2 to 3 cloves garlic, chopped

4 to 8 ounces of roasted green chiles, chopped (I prefer pasilla chiles)

Guacamole, sour cream, and salsa or pico de gallo

Place the whole block of squirrels in a large stockpot with homemade chicken broth and water to cover. Simmer the pot contents for 4 to 6 hours, or until

FROM FIELD TO TABLE

the meat starts getting tender, and the fragrance in the kitchen is appetizing and lacks any hint of "pine."

After simmering, remove the meat from the bone. Shred or chop the meat. You really can't over-process squirrel meat, as it's quite resilient and can handle all sorts of treatments. If you're familiar with Mexican food, go for a "carnitas" texture.

Sauté onion and garlic in olive oil in a large skillet. Add chiles, simmer, then add squirrel meat. Heat and stir ingredients at low to medium temperature for about 10 minutes.

Heat corn tortillas on the comal or griddle with a little canola or corn oil. Place roughly 3 tablespoons of the meat mixture in each tortilla, enough that it rolls easily. Roll into a "squirrelito" and secure with toothpick. Heat oil in skillet and fry squirrelitos until tortillas are crispy. Drain on paper towels and serve. Have bowls of salsa, guacamole, and sour cream ready to accent your creation!

Chicken Broth

1 to 2 tablespoons cumin

3 to 4 bay leaves

4 cloves garlic

3 cubes Knorr Tomato Bouillon with chicken (available at Mexican food stores)

1 whole chicken (or even leftover rotisserie carcass with some skin, fat, and meat remaining)

Water to cover

Mix ingredients and simmer for 3 hours.

Sweet and Sour Rabbit

2 rabbits, cut into serving-sized pieces

½ cup flour

Salt and pepper

2 tablespoons vegetable or olive oil

3 tablespoons brown sugar

2 tablespoons cider vinegar

2 teaspoons soy sauce

1 clove garlic

1 can pineapple chunks

½ green pepper, cut into 1-inch squares

1 small onion, cut into quarters

Place flour, salt, and pepper in a paper or plastic bag, add rabbit pieces, and shake until the rabbit is well coated. Place pieces in a pan and brown in hot oil. Combine pieces and all remaining ingredients and simmer for 1 hour or until tender, or place in 350-degree oven and bake for 2 hours.

Simple Fried Rabbit or Squirrel

1 rabbit or squirrel, cut into quarters
2 tablespoons oil
1 teaspoon pepper
1 teaspoon seasoned salt
1 teaspoon garlic powder
½ cup water, chicken broth, or wine

Place seasonings in a bag with rabbit and shake (or season to taste). Place seasoned rabbit in skillet with hot oil and brown. After rabbit is browned, add water, broth, or wine to skillet, turn down the heat, cover, and simmer for 45 minutes to an hour or until rabbit is tender.

Southern Fried Rabbit

1 rabbit, cut into quarters
Vinegar
Salt water
Salt
Pepper
Flour

Soak rabbit for about 2 hours, using enough vinegar and salt water to cover the meat. Take out and pat dry. Salt, pepper, and flour the meat. Put it in a hot skillet with enough oil for frying. Fry until the meat is a rich brown, and when you stick it with a knife, you don't see any blood. Make a gravy with the drippings.

Broiled Squirrel

One or more skinned and cleaned squirrels
Salt
Pepper
Fat
Lemon juice

Rub cleaned squirrels with salt and pepper. Brush with fat and place on hot broiling rack. Broil 40 minutes, turning frequently and basting with drippings every 10 minutes. Serve with gravy from drippings and season with 1 to 2 tablespoons of lemon juice.

Rabbit or Squirrel Pie

3 pounds of rabbit or squirrel,
cut into quarters

6 tablespoons butter, divided

1 teaspoon salt

Generous grinding of pepper

1 bay leaf

1 small onion, sliced

½ cup chopped celery

½ cup peas

1 cup finely diced potatoes

3 tablespoons flour

¼ cup light cream

A dash of cayenne pepper

Pastry crust or biscuit dough

2–3 cups chicken or other broth, divided

Brown meat in Dutch oven or skillet using butter, then add enough water or broth to cover meat. Season to taste, adding the bay leaf and onion. Cover and let simmer for 1½ to 2 hours on very low heat or until the meat is very tender. Remove bay leaf and discard. Remove meat, pick the meat from the bones, and place it in a casserole dish. Cook the vegetables in the broth in the Dutch oven or skillet for about 10 minutes, then remove and scatter over the meat in the casserole dish.

In a separate saucepan, melt remaining butter and stir in flour, cooking over low heat until bubbly and smooth. Slowly pour in 1 to 1½ cups of broth and the light cream, and cook until slightly thickened. Add a dash of cayenne pepper and check to see if additional salt and pepper is needed. Pour over the vegetables and meat.

If you are using pastry crust, roll it about ⅛-inch thick, place over casserole, and cut gashes for steam to escape. Bake at 400 degrees for about 20 minutes or until the crust is browned. If you are using biscuit dough, roll the dough about ½-inch thick and cut into rounds. Place these on top of the casserole and bake at 425 degrees for about 30 minutes or until the biscuits are browned.

Hunter's Delight

½ cup chopped bacon

2 medium onions

2 cloves garlic, crushed

1 stewed tomato, chopped

1 teaspoon thyme

¼ cup flour

Biscuit dough

1 large rabbit or 2 large squirrels

Fry all the ingredients with the bacon in a Dutch oven (except the meat) until brown, then add the meat, salt and pepper to taste, and continue to cook.

Brown the flour in an iron frying pan. Stir constantly to avoid burning, but make sure it is browned well. Add it to the meat with enough water to make it soupy. Stew it down until the meat is falling off the bone and the liquid is thick.

Now make biscuit dough and drop small-sized biscuits over the top of the stew. Stick it all in an oven preheated to 400 degrees and bake 20–30 minutes until the biscuits are done.

Brunswick Stew

5 pounds of squirrel or rabbit, cut into quarters

Bacon drippings

3 sliced onions

Meaty hambone (if handy)

1 tablespoon salt

¼ teaspoon black pepper

2 quarts of canned tomatoes drained (save the liquid)

Chicken bouillon (optional)

4 medium-sized potatoes, peeled and diced

½ teaspoon cayenne pepper

A liberal pinch of thyme and parsley flakes

2 cups fresh or frozen lima beans

2 cups fresh or frozen corn

2 cups okra

Fine dry bread crumbs

Pat the meat dry with paper towels, then brown in hot fat in a Dutch oven or skillet. Season with salt and pepper, then add onions and continue to brown for another minute or two. Using either chicken bouillon or liquid from the drained tomatoes and some water, add enough liquid to cover the meat. Add meaty hambone if you have it. Cover and simmer on low heat until the meat is tender. Remove the meat from the bones and cut into pieces, then return it to the liquid along with the tomatoes, potatoes, cayenne, thyme, and parsley. Cook for an additional 30 minutes on low heat, then add the rest of the vegetables and continue cooking until they are tender but not mushy. If frozen vegetables are used, shorten the cooking time after they have been added. Check seasonings before serving and, if necessary, thicken the stew with fine dry bread crumbs. Don't get carried away with the thickening, as Brunswick stew should be the consistency of a thick soup. It usually is served in soup plates with corn bread.

Glossary

anseriform: Birds of the order Anseriformes, which includes ducks and geese. These birds are characterized by their aquatic lifestyle and webbed feet.

bajada: The slopes at the base of a mountain that transition into the plains below.

bosque: Spanish word for "woodland," used to describe the thick forest in a floodplain or along a river or creek.

cere: The soft skin around the base of the upper mandible, which often includes the eye and nostril.

charadriiform: Small- to medium-sized birds of the order Charadriiformes, most of which live near water and eat invertebrates or other small animals. Some are wading birds, while others are pelagic (sea birds).

columbiform: Birds of the order Columbiformes, all of which are dove- and pigeon-like. These birds are characterized by having four toes, short legs, and relatively small heads.

covey: A flock of birds, usually used in reference to a group of quail.

crepuscular: Active during the twilight hours; i.e., early morning and late evening.

dimorphic or **dimorphism:** The physical difference exhibited between sexes of the same species.

disjunct: Broken or fragmented.

diurnal: Active during the day.

dorsum, dorsal, or **dorsally:** Referring to the back or top.

emergent vegetation: Plants such as cattails, rushes, reeds, and waterlilies, which are rooted in the water and protrude from its surface.

flush: To take flight or run, or to make to take flight; to drive from cover or hiding.

flyway: The route traveled by birds while migrating or moving to particular areas such as feeding, loafing, or roosting sites.

galliform, gallinaceous: Chicken-like birds of the order Galliformes, characterized by their ground-dwelling and ground-feeding habits, heavy bodies, strong legs, and broad, powerful wings.

incisors: The two (often modified) foremost teeth of the upper and lower jaw. These are greatly enlarged in rodents and lagomorphs.

loafing site: An area used by wildlife while inactive or resting. These sites are often employed during the inactive midday hours.

magnum load: Loads for firearms characterizing ballistic qualities beyond the standards. This may be heavier shot and/or powder charges and increased velocities.

mandible: The jaw. The lower mandible is the lower jaw, and the upper mandible is the upper jaw.

nocturnal: Active at night.

ochre: Yellow-orange in color.

precocious: Animals that exhibit advanced development at birth, such as being fully furred, or having eyes open.

rufous: Yellow-pink to reddish in color.

sky island: A term used to describe the forested mountain ranges of southeastern Arizona and northern Mexico that are surrounded by desert or grassland habitats. Like islands in an ocean, these mountains offer habitats that are not found in the areas that surround them.

subequatorial: Occurring below or south of the equator.

supraequatorial: Occurring above or north of the equator.

taxonomy: A word that comes from the Greek words *taxis*, meaning "arrangement," and *nomia*, meaning "method." This is the biological discipline of classifying and organizing living things. The taxonomy of a species identifies its place in the classification of all known species and demonstrates its relationship to other organisms.

tubercle: A bump, nodule, or wart-like protuberance.

type specimen: The animal or plant on which the description of the species was based; typically, the original specimen collected of a particular animal or plant.

vent: The area near or surrounding the anus.

ventral or **ventrally:** Referring to the belly or underside.

Bibliography

American Ornithologists' Union. 1998. *Check-list of North American Birds*, 7th ed. Washington, D.C.: American Ornithologists' Union.

Baird, S. F. 1857. Mammals. In Reports of Explorations and Surveys, Ascertain the Most Practicable and Economical Route for a Railroad from the Mississippi River to the Pacific Ocean. Made Under the Direction of the Secretary of War in 1853–6. 8(1): xii–xlvii + 1-1757 + 43 pls.

Bent, A. C. 1932. *Life Histories of North American Gallinaceous Birds*. Smithsonian Institution Bulletin 162.

Best, T. L. 1993. *Lepus alleni*. Mammalian Species. American Society of Mammalogists, 424:1–8.

Best, T. L. 1995. *Sciurus nayaritensis*. Mammalian Species. American Society of Mammalogists, 492:1–5.

Best, T. L. 1996. *Lepus californicus*. Mammalian Species. American Society of Mammalogists, 530:1–10.

Best, T. L., and S. Riedel. 1995. *Sciurus arizonensis*. Mammalian Species. American Society of Mammalogists, 496:1–5.

Brown, D. E. 1984. *Arizona's Tree Squirrels*. Phoenix: Arizona Game and Fish Department.

Brown, D. E. 1985. *Arizona's Wetlands and Waterfowl*. Tucson: Univ. of Arizona Press.

Brown, D. E. 1989. *Arizona Game Birds*. Tucson: Univ. of Arizona Press.

Brown, D. E., K. B. Clark, R. D. Babb, and G. Harris. 2011. *An Analysis of Masked Bobwhite Collection Locales and Habitat Characteristics*. In *Quail Management Proceedings*. Quail VII-15. Allen Press: Lawrence, Kansas.

Brown, R. W. 1954. *Composition of Scientific Words*. Baltimore: Reese Press.

Camp, R. R. 1983. *Game Cookery in America and Europe*. Los Angeles: HP Books.

Chapman, J. A. 1975. *Sylvilagus nuttallii*. Mammalian Species. American Society of Mammalogists, 56:1–3.

Chapman, J. A. 1980. *Sylvilagus floridanus*. Mammalian Species. American Society of Mammalogists, 136:1–8.

Chapman, J. A., and G. R. Willner. 1978. *Sylvilagus audubonii*. Mammalian Species. American Society of Mammalogists, 106:1–4.

Corman, T. E., and C. Wise-Gervais. 2005. *Arizona Breeding Bird Atlas*. Albuquerque: Univ. of New Mexico Press.

Dunn, J. L., and J. Alderfer. 2008. *Field Guide to the Birds of Western North America*. Washington, D. C.: National Geographic Society.

Engel-Wilson, R., and W. P. Kuvlesky Jr. 2002. "Arizona Quail: Species in Jeopardy?" In *Proceeding of the Fifth National Quail Symposium*, Texas Parks and Wildlife Department, Austin: 1–7.

Gotch, A. F. 1995. *Latin Names Explained: A Guide to the Scientific Classification of Reptiles, Birds and Mammals*. New York: Facts On File Inc.

Hoffmeister, D. F. 1986. *Mammals of Arizona.* Tucson: Univ. of Arizona Press and Arizona Game and Fish Department.

Johnsgard, P. A. 1975. *North American Game Birds of Upland and Shoreline.* Lincoln: Univ. of Nebraska Press.

Johnsgard, P. A. 1983. *Cranes of the World: Sandhill Crane* (Grus canadensis). Lincoln: Univ. of Nebraska Press.

Kneeland, M. C., and J. L. Koproswski. 1995. "Potential Predators of Chiricahua Fox Squirrels (*Sciurus nayaritensis chiricahuae*)." *Southwestern Naturalist* 40 (3).

Koproswski, J. L. and M. C. Corse. 2001. "Food Habits of the Chiricahua Fox Squirrel (*Sciurus nayaritensis chiricahuae*)." *Southwestern Naturalist* 46 (1): 62–65.

Koproswski, J. L., and M. C. Corse. 2005. "Time Budgets, Activity Periods, and Behavior of Mexican Fox Squirrels." *Journal of Mammalogy* 86 (5): 947–952.

Mickler, E. M. 1986. *White Trash Cooking.* Berkeley: Ten Speed Press.

Nash, D. J., and R. N. Seaman. 1977. *Sciurus aberti.* Mammalian Species. American Society of Mammalogists, 80:1–5.

Nelson, E. W. 1907. "Descriptions of New North American Rabbits." In *Proceedings of the Washington Biological Society* (20): 81–84.

Nelson, E. W. 1909. "Rabbits of North America." *North American Fauna* 29.

Parton, W. S. 1996. *Wingshooter's Guide to Arizona.* Belgrade, Montana: Wilderness Adventures Press.

Parton, W. S. 2008. *Bond of Passion: Living with and Training your Hunting Dog.* Oracle, Arizona: Casa Cielo Press.

Pasch, B. S., and J. L. Koprowski. 2005. "Correlates of Vulnerability in Chiricahua Fox Squirrels." USDA Forest Service Proceedings, RMRS-P-36: 426–428.

Pasch, B. S., and J. L. Koprowski. 2006. "Annual Cycles in Body Mass and Reproduction of Chiricahua Fox Squirrels (*Sciurus nayaritensis chiricahuae*)." *Southwestern Naturalist* 51 (4): 531–535.

Pasch, B. S., and J. L. Koprowski. 2006. "Sex Differences in Space Use of Chiricahua Fox Squirrels." *Journal of Mammalogy* 87 (2): 380–386

Rue, L. L. 1973. *Game Birds of North America.* New York: Outdoor Life/Harper and Rowe.

Smith, C. S. 2000. *Field Guide to Upland Birds and Waterfowl.* Belgrade, Montana: Wilderness Adventures Press.

Steele, M. A. 1998. *Tamiasciurus hudsonicus.* Mammalian Species. American Society of Mammalogists, 586:1–9.

Tacha, T. C., and C. E. Braun. 1994. *Migratory Shore and Upland Game Bird Management in North America.* International Association of Fish and Wildlife Agencies.

Taylor, W. P., C. T. Vorhies, and P. B. Lister. 1935. "The Relation of Jack Rabbits to Grazing in Southern Arizona." *Journal of Forestry* 33:490–498.

Tinsley, R. 1976. *All About Small-Game Hunting in America.* New York: Winchester Press.

Verts, J. B., and S. D. Gehman. 1991. "Activity and Behavior of Free-living *Sylvilagus nuttallii.*" *Northwest Science* 65 (5): 231–237.

Vorhies, C. T., and W. P. Taylor. 1933. *The Life Histories and Ecology of Jack Rabbits* Lepus alleni *and* Lepus californicus spp., *in Relation to Grazing in Arizona.* Tucson: Univ. of Arizona, Agricultural Experiment Station Technical Bulletin 49:471–587.

Williams, B. O. 2001. *Hunting the Quails of North America.* Minocqua, Wisconsin: Willow Creek Press.

Zink, R. M., and R. C. Blackwell. 1998. "Molecular Systematics of the Scaled Quail Complex (Genus *Callipepla*)." *Auk* 115 (2): 394–403.

Index